SLUT

SLUT

A PLAY and GUIDEBOOK for COMBATING
SEXISM and SEXUAL VIOLENCE

Edited by KATIE CAPPIELLO and MEG McINERNEY
Introduction by JENNIFER BAUMGARDNER

AFTERWORD WITH CAROL GILLIGAN

THE FEMINIST PRESS
AT THE CITY UNIVERSITY OF NEW YORK
NEW YORK CITY

Published in 2015 by the Feminist Press
at the City University of New York
The Graduate Center
365 Fifth Avenue, Suite 5406
New York, NY 10016

feministpress.org

First printing February 2015

Cover and text design by Drew Stevens

Library of Congress Cataloging-in-Publication Data
SLUT : a play and guidebook for combating sexism and
sexual violence / edited by Katie Cappiello and Meg
McInerney ; introduction by Jennifer Baumgardner ;
afterword with Carol Gilligan.
      pages cm
   ISBN 978-1-55861-870-1 (paperback) — ISBN 978-1-55861-871-8
(ebook)
1. American drama—Women authors. 2. Sexism—Drama. 3.
Sex crimes—Drama. 4. Sex role—Drama. 5. Young women—
Crimes against—Drama. 6. Sex crimes—United States. I.
Cappiello, Katie, editor. II. McInerney, Meg, editor.
  PS628.W6S58 2015
812'.60809287—dc23
                                        2014046270

For our loving parents Jane and Mike Cappiello
and Claudia and Maury McInerney.

For our siblings, our students, and our teachers.

For Jamison and Jason.

And for Celia Rose T. Fitzgerald who
inspires us every day to "do fancy things for
the world" and whose life and memory, in
so many ways, brought us here.

"Every woman who appears wrestles with the forces that would have her disappear. She struggles with the forces that would tell her story for her, or write her out of the story, the genealogy, the rights of man, the rule of law. The ability to tell your own story, in words or images, is already a victory, already a revolt."

—Rebecca Solnit, *Men Explain Things to Me*

Contents

Why StopSlut?

JENNIFER BAUMGARDNER

I don't recall when I first heard the word slut, but by the time I was twelve, I knew intuitively and immediately what it connoted: a girl who was sexual and worthless. I remember I was running around the gym in a stinky polyester Agassiz Tigers gym suit. Another seventh grader ran up to me and said, "Jenny, your sister's a slut. She had sex at Bob's party over the weekend."

Up until that moment, I had thought of my four-teen-year-old sister, Andrea, as basically like me, but with clearer skin and better curling iron skills. We were adolescent Baumgardners—meaning tall, awkward, smart brace-faces. Suddenly, because of the sex, Andrea was mature, wanton, and trashy, ready to do it with anyone. Although it made no sense, I accepted this new version of reality.

As it turned out, the "sex" that branded Andrea a slut was not consensual. She was at the party trying alcohol for the first time. When she retreated to a bedroom to lie down and sober up, her boyfriend's best friend followed her in and decided to have sex with her. Nauseous and reeling, she said no and pushed him away as best she could.

Word spread immediately throughout her high school and my junior high and to the neighboring schools, too. Girls distanced themselves from Andrea to distance themselves from the word slut—to convey that they were definitely *not* the kind of girls you could do anything like that to, *not* the kind of girls whom no one feels compelled to care about or help. Meanwhile, boys got *too* close. They preyed on her, running their hands up her shirt as she passed by, pulling her into rooms at parties. Being a slut meant any guy who felt entitled had license to touch her.

When Andrea graduated from Fargo South High four years later, she had been first-chair viola in the orchestra, a near straight-A student, on the basketball team that took state, class speaker at her graduation, and had gotten into every elite college she applied to. Still, as she told me recently, none of those accomplishments mattered, because she was "just a slut." Nothing was bigger than that identity.

It took Andrea and me many years to realize that she had been raped and then blamed for it, a process I now think of as "slutting" and is more commonly referred to as "slut shaming."

Slut shaming means to degrade women's and girls' sexuality and then use it to justify harassment and rape. With slut shaming, girls are made to feel guilty for their sexuality and punished for their sexual power or their desire for sexual attention. It is a way for our culture to justify rampant sexual violence. The slut is the scapegoat of sex.

As was the case with my sister, young girls are

often called sluts before they even learn the meaning of the word. Being called a slut (or doing what they can to avoid being labeled that way) is often a girl's first experience of being second-class. Being slut shamed is an initiation, a kind of hazing into mature womanhood that shatters a girl's sense, if she ever had it, that she might escape that particular female humiliation. Our cultural silence around it is a powerful socialization tool—we all normalize females as less than.

I made sure not to be a slut in high school. It wasn't hard because I was terrified of sex and ran with a musical theater crowd (read: the boys are gay, the girls are too worried about preserving their ability to belt "Macavity" to use intoxicants). In a way, I tried to protect myself from my sister's experience, all the while telling myself that it wouldn't happen to me because I was strong and different. I pictured myself as exceptional because the reality—that I too could be raped and treated as worthless by my community—was too frightening to acknowledge.

It was an immense relief to go to college in 1988 because finally I had language, tools, and a community with which I could talk about these kinds of experiences. Andrea and I could name what happened to her at that party for what it was: rape. Literally dozens of my friends had similar stories. I was aflame, in a crazy, conflicted, college feminist (outrage + miniskirt) way, with an urgent need to change things. I fought with the philosophy majors at frat parties about whether rape was "natural." I scheduled meetings with deans, angrily accusing them of not caring about student safety and covering up the "real" rape statistics on our campus. Inspired by students at Brown, my friends and I anonymously published a "castration list"—the names of male students that had raped women we knew—and hung it in the bathroom in the student union. We didn't change much, but action and discussion felt good—healing, even. We had a forum to express our rage and protest injustice. We had a chance to tell our truths and begin to narrate a reality that coincided with our actual lives.

The reality is that there are certain feminist issues that persist despite the appearance of universal outrage. Those issues often connect to women's sexuality and the material fact that the capacity to give life or not give life funnels through our bodies (which also house our minds and souls). We embody the ambivalence that patriarchal culture (which is to say the culture we've known for the last 5,000 or so years) has about the ultimate female power.

Today, I am often a keynote speaker at Take Back the Night events on campuses around the country. It's déjà vu all over again. We march, we acknowledge the impact of sexual violence, we chant "yes means yes/no means no/whatever we wear/wherever we go"—everything, down to the statistics, remains the same. Between one in five American women will experience rape or attempted rape in her life, according to the Department of Justice, and many men and boys will, too. I wonder, will my children—ages five and nine—also attend identical Take Back the Night marches?

It pains me to see how much student activism there is and yet how little the reality of rape and slut shaming changes. That is why I'm so grateful to this book and the play contained within it. Duane de Four analyzes the myths of socially mandated male sexual aggression, Leora Tanenbaum insightfully documents how slut shaming has increased in virulence in the age of the Internet, and a wide range of young people share their stories of experiencing slut culture. In sum, this project has delivered me from an overwhelming state of defeat. I first saw *SLUT* in New York City in 2013. My reactions were so complex, it has taken me fifteen more viewings to begin to unpack them. The play opens with five girls dancing around in a locker room—teasing, frank, sweet, hilarious—and having fun as well as playing with their burgeoning sexuality. Immediately, the audience has to confront their feelings about girls and their bodies—and most are provoked to judging the girls for being too thin, not thin enough, too sexy, or too sexless.

In the play, as in life, the girls call each other sluts—but they mean "sexy" and "hot" and "powerful" and "daring." But then something happens to demonstrate how far we are from being able to deploy the term slut in a way that benefits girls and women. Every time I see it, by the end of the play, many in the audience are crying. I've seen eighty-year-old women connect to childhood rapes and teenagers speak movingly about the betrayals they face currently. As people exit the theater, there is visible relief and joy. *SLUT* literally provides catharsis—release from strong, repressed emotions and pain, as well as the integration of pieces of us long ago exiled.

Sexuality for girls and boys is defined by our culture, as is pleasure. Boys are expected to always want to have sex, with very little space to say no or not now. Meanwhile, girls are expected to be sexually alluring, which then shifts blame for the violence perpetrated by rapists and molesters onto women. Their desire to be perceived as attractive is conflated with accepting violation. *SLUT*, the StopSlut Movement, and the powerful essays in this book help young people reflect on these social messages and supports them to make good choices about how they want to experiment.

The beginning of challenging rape culture is empathizing with, as this play lets you, the human being (in this play, Joey Del Marco) who is called a slut—as well as the conflicts of every single perspective dramatized in the course of *SLUT*. It dramatizes necessary conversations rarely seen (let alone had) before: between a sister and her brother who looked out the window and let it happen, between Joey's best friend and her feminist mother, and a brief but wrenching moment between Joey and her dad. Joey's desire to protect her father from pain and her fear that he's disappointed in her exactly mirrors my sister's experience in keeping silent, although it means she didn't get the support she needed and deserved from her parents.

The play frames the full range of our reactions and all of our shameful doubts, things we would never want to admit to thinking about that girl (all those girls), the part of us that says (even if we were raped in the same way), "What the hell was she thinking? Put on some clothes!! Are you insane?" The play's brilliance is that it lets that woman hatred which we have internalized fill the theater and also keeps leading us back to this very human, all too relatable character and her all too relatable rape. And when we finally tune into her, it is perfectly clear what happened and who is to blame. We feel compassion for Joey Del Marco—and we begin to feel compassion for ourselves. Our allegiance to each other within a larger movement for sexual freedom and justice is strengthened by this experience.

And there couldn't be a better moment for this intervention. For the first time, we have the leadership of President Obama as well as a huge surge in student activism exerting historic pressure on colleges to deal with their rape problem or risk being out of compliance with Title IX. This work has the power to frame issues in a crucial way that sensitizes people who make policy. As writer, rape survivor, and self-defense teacher Anastasia Higginbotham, put it: "I left the theater thinking: Damn, this is going to work! Rape culture will be challenged."

No one is born knowing how to have sex. Fumbling needs to happen as we all learn what it means to have bodies and sexuality, love and acceptance. This play, this book, the voices and activism contained within, give me hope that future generations might fumble without hurting themselves or others. "Damn," I think about this StopSlut Movement, "This is going to work. We can make it work."

We owe it to ourselves to make it work.

Reality Check From Young Voices

Well, Then Every Girl Has Been Raped . . .
Sonia, 15

Hi. I'm Sonia. I'm fifteen and a sophomore in high school in a small town in Pennsylvania.

At the beginning of my freshman year I was fourteen and I had a new boyfriend. I was excited—honestly all I wanted at that point in my life was someone to cuddle and watch *Grey's Anatomy* with. For a little while, everything was really cute. He introduced me to his parents, held my hand in school. Actually, all of my friends thought we were perfect. We had been dating for a little over a month, when I asked him what he wanted for his sixteenth birthday. All he wanted from me was a blow job.

He made this clear to me in the weeks leading up to his birthday. I'd say, "Hey, what do you want for your birthday?" and he'd say, "Head." I had never seen a dick before, and I didn't particularly want to. I was dreading it for weeks, but I mean, I knew what I had to do.

On his birthday we left school at lunch to go to his house. I pleaded with him for us to just go to a restaurant or something instead but he got angry and said it was his fucking birthday and just walked away from me, so I ran after him because I didn't want him to be mad. When we got to his place he led me straight into his bedroom and just took his pants off. I stalled for as long as possible without directly saying "no," but then I just stopped. I said I didn't want to. Not now. I had to go back to school. Not now.

He was furious. He screamed until there were tears streaming down my face and then he told me to go and he slammed the door and I ran back to school sobbing.

I told one of my best friends what happened when I got back to school. I was supposed to wait for him to get out of his class at the end of the day and go over to his house again. I didn't know whether or not I should wait for him or just go home. I knew he'd be more angry if I left. And she said to me, "Is it worth it? I mean, he's gonna be so angry. It's his birthday. You should wait." What she was really saying to me, though, was, "You should just get over it and suck his dick."

And I did.

Because it wasn't worth it to say no to him. But what I was saying wasn't "yes." I wasn't thinking, "I really want to give my boyfriend head because it will make me happy to make him happy." I was thinking, "Fine! I'll give my boyfriend head because I'd rather that than him yell at me again."

And that went on for over a year. There were times when I did genuinely consent, but for the most part, I just did whatever he wanted me to do or let him do whatever he wanted to do to me because in my mind, it wasn't worth it to fight him. Sometimes I would try, but he took my "no" as "convince me." He wouldn't stop touching me. I would grab his hand to try and stop him, but then he would get mad at me for making it seem like he was doing something wrong. I would say no over and over again but he would keep pleading so that eventually it was so unpleasant for me to keep saying no that I just couldn't do it anymore—I would give in. He would say things like, "but I bought you hot chocolate" or, "I would do this for you even if I wasn't feeling like it." He called the week every month when I had my period "blow job week." I was positive though, that if I really said "no" and I really meant it, he would stop.

Then there was the time on his couch, probably about a year or so into our relationship—I don't remember exactly. We were watching TV and I was lying next to him and he turned me toward him. We made out and stuff for a couple minutes, but I did not want to have sex with him right then on his couch. I turned away from him. He turned me back over. I said *"Stop"* sort of casually because I didn't want to alarm him. He pulled my leggings down to my knees. I said, "Not right here—not right now, can we at least go in your room? I don't want to do this." He did not stop. I went numb. He leaned over me and put his hands on the back of the couch. He was not looking at me. But his dog was in the room—looking right at me. I made eye contact with the dog, and in some ways I've never been able to leave that moment: silent, on his couch, as he repeatedly and painfully thrust into me, just looking at his dog.

He finished. I pulled my leggings up and I don't

remember what happened next, but I ended up on his bathroom floor, shaking.

I wish I could tell you that I realized at the time that there was something wrong with that day. With all of it, really. But that's the thing—I didn't. I didn't get him out of my life until a month after his seventeenth birthday. If you were to read my journal, though, you'd see that for almost the whole time I was with him I was writing things like "I am so trapped," or "My relationship is toxic and I have no control."

I think the reason why I didn't leave him on his sixteenth birthday and every day after that was because everything around me was telling me that it was okay. After we broke up, I started going to therapy because I was struggling with anxiety and self-harm—things I had not struggled with at all prior to my relationship with him. Something I learned in therapy is that you are not actually giving consent unless you feel free to say no and you still say yes. So many times with him, I had not felt free to say no.

In therapy, really recently actually, I realized that that day on his couch was rape. When I said to one of my best friends, "You know, technically speaking he raped me, " she laughed. She laughed and said, "Well, then every girl has been raped." Sadly, I know a lot of girls who have been pressured into doing things that they didn't want to do, girls who have been coerced, or intimidated, or guilted, who have felt like they had no other option. Girls who have said no but then gone silent and limp. Girls who have had boyfriends who blur all the lines until they aren't sure of anything at all—until they don't believe themselves. Girls who would rather accept that they are "crazy" or "overreacting" or that it "wasn't that bad" than accept what happened to them. Girls like me.

And none of these girls, none of us, feels entitled to the pain that comes with any sexual assault because what happens to us is so "normal." We are all "normal." And none of these guys are ever held accountable because what they do is "normal."

I go to school with this boy. I see him every day. I see him happy, laughing with his friends. I see him with his new girlfriend. I walk by him in the hallways. He accidentally brushes my shoulder at parties. He will never be held accountable for what he did to me. I have nothing. I'm just a bitter ex-girlfriend who "childishly," as it has been put to me, refuses to say hi to her ex-boyfriend.

I'm sick of it being "normal." I'm sick of the silence. I'm sick and I'm tired of being scared to say anything about what happened to me because I'm so afraid that no one would ever believe me because he was my boyfriend and because I stayed with him for so long. But I've been doing some research, and apparently 28 percent of rapists are intimates of their victims. So really, though most of the time it feels like it, I'm not alone. I should not have to be afraid of the repercussions for me in my school and social life that would result from coming forward. But I am—every girl in my position is too. I am sick of that being our reality.

And I really hope you are too.

What Are We Learning from J-Hova?
Odley, 18

When I was a little kid, starting at about seven years old, I loved to listen to music and watch music videos. I loved hip-hop, R & B, a little bit of rap, pop, rock—basically everything. As long as it was catchy, I loved it. I would sing along to these songs having no clue what the artists were singing and rapping about. I would watch the music videos and see nothing but African American women in bikinis dancing, having a good time, and getting attention from lots of guys. One song I really enjoyed was "Big Pimpin'" by Jay-Z. Damn, that cruise ship looked fun! All the beautiful women, their amazing swim suits, smiling, dancing around the men while champagne was poured on their faces. It seemed great to me at the time. I was a young girl just dancing to the beat, drooling over the glamorous lifestyle, and laughing—completely unaware of what I was really hearing and seeing.

As I got older, I started to actually listen to the lyrics and I began to understand what was being said. Just recently, I was watching Throwback Jams on MTV and I heard a familiar beat, I looked up and it was "Big Pimpin'" big and bold on my TV. I got up and started dancing, rapping the lyrics along with Hova: *You know I thug em, fuck em, love em, leave em, cause I don't fuckin need em, Take em out the hood, keep em lookin good but I don't fuckin feed em. First time they fuss I'm breezin, Talkin bout, 'what's the reasons?' I'm a pimp in every sense of the word, bitch. Better trust than believe em, and*

REALITY CHECK FROM YOUNG VOICES

I was suddenly just like *whoa*—okay that's kind of messed up, but kept on jamming to the song. Then I heard *Heart cold as assassins, I got no passion, I got no patience, and I hate waitin,' ho get yo ass in and let's ride.*

I stopped and thought, "Ho?" I looked up at the TV to make sure these women in the video reacted to what was just said but, no, they were still just dancing. I sat back down and wondered, did anyone hear this but me? And the song continued to play. It wasn't until the end that I realized this whole entire thing is about spending money, playing women, abusing women, and treating women as less than human.

The "lucky" women in this video are just things—toys and scenery—not people. Their self-worth is completely diminished. Yeah, it's great to be sexy, but in these videos the women have no control. Girls are taught to want to be like these women because, come on, who wouldn't want to be partying with Jay-Z on his badass yacht? And what guy doesn't want to be Jigga with a rap career, and cash, and bottles of Cristal, and a boat full of half-naked sluts, right? There is a very unhealthy male to female dynamic being modeled in these videos by celebrities we worship.

In the media, African American women are often portrayed as voluptuous and sexual with "ratchet," ghetto attitudes and three baby daddies. And music videos pack the biggest punch against young women of color. Instead of rapping about our beauty and our strength, male recording artists call us "sexy bitches" or "fine-ass hos." Instead of showing us affection, they're pouring alcoholic beverages on our faces, throwing cash at us, telling us to "play with the dick in the truck." As an African American young woman, I have to stand up and fight against this. I should not feel like I have to mimic the women in these videos to get the attention I want from a boy I like. And boys should not expect us to act that way. Maybe if the media didn't portray us as hos, bitches, big-booty Judys, or sluts, we would get a little more respect and have a little more room to just be who we are.

You Watch Porn
Fred, 13

"You watch porn?"

Lenny asks me with one of his very signature smiles, the kind of smile that almost makes you feel bad. It's a smile that feels equivalent to being laughed at. I don't really want to answer Lenny's question. Talking about porn makes me uncomfortable, I start to feel tense. Plus there's a bunch of other guys in the room—it's sixth grade and I just started hanging out with this group. We're at Alex's house, and I'm sitting on the couch with Alex, Jack, Tom, and Doug. Lenny is sitting on a chair, staring at me with his smile, waiting for an answer. He probably knows I don't really want to talk about porn, but that doesn't matter much to him. Lenny is very persistent. Once he has an idea there's no stopping him; once he has a question, he wants his answer. I try to just mumble a response. "What?" Lenny says, and then he repeats himself. "Do you watch porn?"

I started watching porn halfway through fifth grade. I had just begun middle school, and befriended a lot of kids in seventh and eighth grade. Sometimes when I hung out with them they would make jokes about the porn they watched, referencing certain sites. After a little bit, I decided to Google some of these sites and was pretty shocked. I wasn't shocked because the videos contained breasts, vaginas, and penises. I expected that. I was shocked by the realization that these porn videos seemed to take place in their very own world, with their own rules and mentality. I had entered a world where instead of referring to the women by name, they were referred to by a combination of their hair color, skin color, and the added words slut or whore. I had entered a world where every girl is recorded saying she "wants it," and "craves cum." It was a world where, after each girl was "fucked," she would blow a kiss to the camera, and the screen would simply fade to black—happily ever after. It was a strange world, and even then I knew I disagreed with most of it. But I still continued to watch.

Lots of days, after coming home, I would Google porn videos, feel fine watching them, and then feel really bad after. It was like marathoning an awful TV show, where you felt a strange addictiveness watching, and then like crap when you finished. I thought it would be easier to not actually think about what I was watching when I watched porn, and decided I would separate my normal self from my porn-watching self completely. I was very secretive about it, telling nobody. This was the opposite of guys like Lenny and Alex. So many days after school I sat listening to them describe the porn they watched or even sometimes the porn other guys watched. I remember Alex saying to me, "Lenny likes big girls, he was watching videos of these fat girls." Alex would never say that directly to Lenny. Everyone feared Lenny. Alex would always say how he hated Lenny and yet he would still let him come over every day after school. Lenny would start wrestling matches and brutalize Alex on his own rug. One time, while we were playing video games, Lenny got Alex in a headlock on the ground, and Alex was actually yelling at him to stop. Lenny didn't feel like it, and so he kept Alex on the ground, twisted Alex's face up, farted on it, and laughed hysterically. Lenny beat the shit out of all of us and he would be smiling, almost menacingly, the whole time. I got really sick of going to Alex's pretty quickly.

So, that takes us back to now, the moment when Lenny asks me if I watch porn, and he is still looking at me, getting kind of angry I haven't answered him yet. I really don't want to talk about porn, but I try to smile and I say, "Yeah, I've watched it a few times." He laughs, the kind of laugh that you know is at you. It's the answer he wanted.

Around four months later, I'm in the school yard talking to Alex and he says how he really doesn't like Lenny anymore. He lists a couple incidents where Lenny came to his house and wrecked things. "Also the thing with Lola," Alex says. "What thing?" I ask him. I think Alex realized it was the first time he spoke out loud about the incident with Lola—he definitely had a reaction on his face like he shouldn't have said what he just said. He didn't really answer at first, but I asked again. He paused, and must have made a conscious decision to really say it this time, and so he did. He said two months ago he and Lenny went to Tom's house. Lola, a girl who goes to our school and was really good friends with Alex and Tom, lived in an apartment above Tom. Tom, Alex, and Lenny all went upstairs to Lola's where she was alone with her dog. Lenny started getting wild and he put his penis on Lola's leg. She was sitting on the couch in her own house with her dog beside her, just hanging out with a bunch of kids she thought were her good friends, and Lenny took his penis and slapped it on her leg because he felt like it while Tom and Alex stood and watched in her living room.

As shocking as everything was, the reactions were maybe the most shocking. After Alex told me, Tom started telling other people. Lola hadn't told anyone. As unfair as it all was, she's the one who felt ashamed. Once the news was out, the reactions from the kids must have been upsetting for her. First there was a lot of disbelief. I overheard kids saying how she'd made it up and some girls in our school said Lola must have wanted it to happen. A group of eighth graders were high-fiving Lenny in the hallways—laughing and smiling. I still remember one of them nodding at Lenny and saying, "Nice."

So I've since learned my attempt to separate my normal self from my porn watching as much as possible, my attempt not to analyze or question anything that happens in those videos, is impossible because it overlaps. In a school like mine where there is a history class on women's suffrage and there are feminist clubs, it's upsetting how quickly things change once a penis is flung around. The distorted world of porn bleeds its way into reality. The worlds can't be separated. The "she wanted it" mentality of porn disgustingly makes its way into the opinions of thirteen-year-olds—even when it's so obvious that she definitely did not "want it."

To be affected by this mentality, you don't even need to click on that first porn video, it's already infected everything else. This women-are-sluts-here-for-your-pleasure mentality does not stay within the confines of a video; it does not fade away like a porn video. Permanent harm is done. It's not fair to anyone. The way guys view sex should not encourage a male-female dynamic that is degrading and deceptive—but that's what's out there at the click of your mouse. And when it remains available the cycle continues. Guys like Lenny keep on coming, most of them learning from the same things and watching similar videos. And so many of us are egging these guys on, we're responsible too. We can't be high-fiving it, or calling it "nice." We're encouraging it.

It's been two years since everything happened. I'm in eighth grade now. And I didn't realize how everything connected until I first saw *SLUT*. I didn't even realize how much Lola must have had to go through. I don't hang out with Lenny and all of those guys anymore. This morning in school though, we had "family living" class and I had to sit right next to Lenny. As a class we started addressing scary incidents, and one girl shared a story about a time when she was harassed by a stranger on the street who told her she had a cute butt. Lenny couldn't stop giggling. I turned to look next to me, and I saw on Lenny's face one of his signature smiles.

My Doorman
Clare, 16

The Rydells in 3E don't like me. They think I'm a slut. Whenever I'm on the elevator with them they glare at me—looking me up and down the whole ride. Sometimes I think I should just take the stairs because, honestly, I don't need them judging me—making me feel like my ass is huge or that I'm a piece of trash. And I'm actually not even allowed to get in the elevator with the Simons anymore. I wouldn't want to anyway. They live on the seventh floor and I can't stand being in a small space with them for that long. I know they think I'm a stupid whore and they don't really try to hide it. Helping to pay for his attorney wasn't really a good way of covering it up.

The lawyers say that as long as he doesn't work in the building anymore and stays away from me it should all be fine. It's not fine though, because I have to deal with my neighbors and their stupid assumptions. No—I'm not an immature sixteen-year-old who freaked out when his hand "accidentally grazed" me. No. They're so ignorant. They don't know that for months leading up to it, when I'd come home from school or rehearsal or babysitting, he'd give me the mail and tell me how beautiful I was becoming, how I was growing up, and then he'd ask for a hug and try to kiss me on the cheek. They don't know that on that day, when no one was home and I forgot my keys, he made me walk up the back stairs with him to my apartment because "the elevator was too slow." I live on the eighth floor. They don't know that he told me I looked "so pretty." They don't know that he wouldn't unlock my door until I gave him a hug. They don't know how tight he hugged me. They don't know that I tried to run into my apartment. They don't know that he grabbed me and pulled me into him and grabbed my breasts and said, "I want a piece of this." They don't know that I waited an hour in my apartment alone, sobbing, waiting for my mom to get home, and that I changed out of my skinny jeans into sweatpants because I was afraid I looked too sexy. They don't know that I haven't worn the clothes I had on that day since—because I don't want to carry a reminder of all this shit around with me. They don't know that because of him I feel less safe in my own home. He was supposed to be guarding my front door, keeping people just like him from getting in. They don't know that because of all of them, I feel guilty. They don't know that because of them, I think I'm a slut. They don't know that I was truly just trying to be polite and nice and friendly to my doorman, I wasn't leading him on, or teasing him, or trying to ruin his life.

They don't know how hard it was to come forward, to tell my parents, and to press charges.

And they all blame me (never him), shame me (never him), hate me (never him), and shoot hurtful looks at me (never him). They pool their money to cover his legal fees; they clearly don't know how hard I plan to fight, how hard I plan to defend myself. They don't know how much I value my right

REALITY CHECK FROM YOUNG VOICES

to be safe in my own home, in my city, in my body. They don't know that no matter how awkward, tired, uncomfortable, ashamed, dirty, foolish, sad, and slutty I feel—I am also proud. I'm proud of myself for not being silent.

That sense of self is what I carry with me when I step into my elevator. That is what I am going to carry with me always.

You a THOT Anyways . . .
Krystal, 17

That
Ho
Over
There

THOT. The first time I heard this word I never thought it'd be as popular as it is now—because of how stupid it is. Amazingly enough, this word has taken over with crazy force. Middle schoolers and forty-three-year-old women know what it means and many of them use it in their daily conversations.

Recently, my mom sent me to pick up my brother in my old neighborhood. I took the bus uptown to the Bronx and this older guy sat next to me. I tried to do homework and I could feel him staring at me, but we didn't talk. Everything was good. Then, as I was about to get off, he asked, "Can I get your number, sexy?" I simply said, "No." It's my number and I'm seventeen, and I don't want to give my info out to some thirty-five-year-old on the uptown bus. "You a THOT anyways," he shouted at me, nice and loud—with this fuck-you-bitch sound to his voice. I caught his eye—shot him a look, but didn't have time to respond, so I just brushed it off and went on my way.

Then it hit me. I was just called a THOT by a thirty-five-year-old guy who doesn't even know who the hell I am. To him, because I rejected him, I was one of "That Ho Over There." I'm a piece of shit, a slut, trash because I didn't want to give a stranger my phone number. He spit degrading words at me to make himself feel like a man again. And it made me want to punch a wall because it never ends.

Truth is, this is what we hear every day. Girls are shamed and humiliated daily by men like that in public places because they don't smile or strut or look in their direction or give out phone numbers. Most of us girls in the Bronx are known as THOTs or hos to the badass, gang-banger niggas on our streets. Just because we're female. Female = THOT.

I have a friend named Anna who lost her virginity at a young age. The guy she lost her virginity to immediately went around telling everyone that he got into her pants. The next week her picture was plastered all over Facebook with the caption: "You're not from the Bronx if you don't know this THOT." It broke my heart. But it's typical. Anna likes guys, so Anna had sex . . . once. Expressing your feeling toward a guy (whether it's "I'm into you" or "I'm not into you") doesn't make you a THOT. Nothing that you ever do makes you a THOT.

That day, I flagged and reported the picture—because that was my friend up there. We've all got to start saying enough is enough.

No You Can't "Join Us for a Little Girl-on-Girl"
Fiona, 15

This might surprise you, but as a member of the
LGBTQ+ community, I'm not immune to slut shaming. Girls can't be attracted to anyone without being
judged. Girls get slut shamed when they show interest in the opposite sex, the same sex, or both sexes.
If she mentions experimenting with both guys and
girls, she's immediately assumed to be a whore. Hey,
she'll hook up with people regardless of their gender, so she'll hook up with anyone, right? Clearly,
she's a slut. And when a girl has only experimented
with girls, guys still find a way to make the relationship seem wrong, dirty, and pornographic.

When I first started dating, I was surprised by
how people treat displays of affection. Anything
more than holding hands tends to gain the attention
of any guy within a ten-foot radius. The most common questions I've been asked are, "Can I watch?"
or "Can I film you?" Yes, you can definitely watch
and get as many videos of us turning around and
walking away as you'd like! The last time I kissed
a girl in public and someone asked if he could film
us, my girlfriend wasn't surprised. She knew the guy
and said this was normal behavior for him. I immediately announced that I was underage, because simply saying "no" isn't good enough. You need a valid
excuse. He didn't let that stop him, though. He tried
to convince me that age didn't matter.

"I can make you famous," he said, "and I'm really
good at this stuff."

Obviously, I didn't care about anything he was saying. What was in it for me? What good could come from a bunch of men fetishizing my relationship? I am not an object. I am not there for some stranger's pleasure. It's amazing to me that my relationship, which doesn't even involve boys or men, still exists through their lens—it's still theirs somehow. On top of that, I am a person, and for someone to ask me to let him into my relationship for his or her voyeuristic purposes is degrading. We have come so far as a society but we still cannot accept that people who differ from our heteronormative societal standards are people, not sex toys.

The only thing I take away from moments like this—moments when I'm shamed, degraded, and burdened because of my sexuality (and I don't just mean my sexual orientation)—is confirmation that there are a lot of guys out there who don't pay much attention to a woman's preference unless they are rejected, in which case the woman becomes a slut or a prude. That's what our culture has taught them.

When Guys Don't Hear No
Alejandro, 17

What defines a slut? Is it the way a girl dresses? Is it the way she behaves? Or is it simply a broad term people use to define someone they don't like? From my perspective, slut seems to mean multiple things depending on the context, and the amazing thing is that often times slut is used just to describe girls in general. For example, at parties I've seen girls get called sluts for anything at all—no matter what they're wearing or what they're doing: "Check out this room full of sluts." Generally, when coming from boys, it's a derogatory term used to label girls and brand them as things to conquer, things to play with, easy to get with, girls who get with many guys, or just dress in a "provocative" manner. It's a tool guys use to show their power and get what they want. As a seventeen-year-old guy, I never really thought much about the word slut. I knew people used it but I didn't always think about the impact. But recently I've realized that the word slut, all the ideas that go along with it, and the fear of being called a slut, make it hard for my female friends to be comfortable in their own skin. I've even seen the word prevent girls from saying "no" and guys from hearing "no."

This is a simple example, but I think it matters and it's one we've probably all seen: Not long ago I was at a party with a couple friends. As it got later and people began to loosen up (get drunk), I observed this kid, probably seventeen, checking out a girl who was hanging out with some friends. As the people around her dispersed and she was left alone, the guy approached her and asked her to dance. She said no and looked away. The guy pushed back: "You're the only girl I want to dance with." She said, "No thanks, seriously." He pushed again, a little more aggressively but trying to be funny, "Come on—no other girl would dance with me—so dance with me," and she replied the same exact way, "No." Annoyed that he was being rejected, this guy tried to act cool, he stood close to the girl and said,

"Well, I'm gonna get something to drink and then we're gonna dance." The girl didn't answer and the boy left. She sat there, not knowing what to do, and looked around the room for her friends. Five minutes later, he returned and asked her to dance again and again and again. She dodged him and walked away as he kept calling after her. Eventually, she found a friend and asked if they could leave.

I know it may seem like not that big of a deal but I think this small incident illustrates a bigger issue. This guy was desperately trying to show his dominance by repeatedly asking the girl to dance in a threatening way. No didn't mean no to this guy. He was up in her face and refused to hear her. It was as if what she was saying didn't matter and what she wanted was secondary to what he wanted. Why? I watched (should I have intervened? I don't know) as this girl was being pressured to do something she clearly didn't want to do to the point of having to leave the party to avoid further confrontation. Why is she the one who feels like she needs to leave? Probably because guys like that call girls sluts, hos, THOTs, and bitches when they don't get their way. Doesn't matter what the girl does, how she's dressed, who she is—that's the punishment for saying "no." Boys at parties these days just try to get with as many girls as they can and do not take no as an answer, and that is the problem. If these guys can't take no for an answer when it comes to a dance—are they taking no for an answer when it comes to heavier stuff? Especially when they have slut in their arsenal?

I've Slutted. Have You?
Danielle, 17

I am guilty of slut shaming. There . . . I said it! And, like those of you reading this, I am someone who cares about making a difference in our world, striving for change in our future, and better attitudes toward girls' sexuality. Many of us believe girls have the right to own and enjoy their sexual selves, but many of us have also both been called a slut and judged someone for their slutty behavior. It's just the truth. We're players in this game. Slut shaming is the way we process and digest the world and other girls and women around us, and sometimes it's how we make ourselves feel better.

I go to this typical Jewish summer camp, where promiscuous behavior is practically encouraged and cultivated. Let's be real, it's literally eight weeks of teenagers breaking the counselors' rules (who in turn egg us on!) in an isolated campsite in the middle of Milford, Pennsylvania—the middle of nowhere. In those two months, with no parental supervision, there are lots of sexual firsts for everyone. The group of girls that I'm friendly with define themselves by their flirtatiousness and sexual interests. There is one girl in particular, Georgia, who is really petite and very pretty, and she doesn't speak that much. She's always hooking up with someone and she lost her virginity before many of the rest of us. She's the dream girl for all the guys at my camp.

So when the annual camp reunion rolled around I wasn't exactly looking forward to seeing all the guys drool over her. I was unable to attend the steamy night-before-reunion sleepover with all of the guys and girls. Disappointed, I spent the night scrolling through Instagram, checking out the great time I'd missed. I came across a picture of Georgia straddling a guy from my camp, a guy I had gotten together with that past summer, Josh. I was jealous and pissed. I vented to my friends about how of course she would do this because she's a slut. A stupid, slutty whore. I hated her.

Then the next day I learned the full story: Everyone got very drunk. Josh and another boy coerced—basically forced—Georgia to give them blow jobs, while others filmed it on their phones. Watching the videos disgusted me. They were pressuring her to take off her clothes and give other guys in the crowd blow jobs—and all of this was going on in the backyard of someone's home! Initially Georgia resisted, very drunkenly, and repeatedly declined these boys' demands. Then she ended up giving in. The scariest part is that her best friends were doing nothing to stop it, but were laughing and encouraging the whole display. My jealously of Georgia faded. In the videos Josh was the one pushing her, a very drunk girl, to perform oral sex. I felt bad. My heart broke—not for him, but for her. Georgia could be any girl I know—even me—any girl caught up in a culture that encourages her to be sexual but then immediately degrades her for it.

This past summer at sleepaway camp, Georgia and I talked for the first time. We were actually having a conversation, and in a sense, became quite friendly. I wonder, how are girls supposed to feel good about themselves and free to explore their sexuality in a healthy and confident manner, if we're not even on each other's sides? How are we supposed to eradicate the negative light on girls' sexuality and empowerment, if we cannot even support one another? It is essentially impossible to move forward in our movement, if we girls don't even have each other's backs. This is why the understanding of, breakdown of, and eventual demolition of the word slut and the negative connotation that comes packaged with girls' sexuality is so important, for us and future generations.

A Letter to Older Girls
Mira, 13

Dear Older Girls,

I am terrified of you. I am in eighth grade and the idea of "older girls" is very nerve-racking. I'm horrified by the idea of you judging me. Judging me for the things I'll say, things I'll do, for who I'll be to you next year when I hit your hallways.

I feel like I already know what's going to happen. And that's what scares me most. It probably happened to all of you at one point freshman year. I'm afraid you're going to look me up and down when I walk through the cafeteria. That you're going to call me a slut for just speaking to an older boy. Or make fun of me for not hooking up the right way or for hooking up too soon or not soon enough. I'm afraid of how you'll label me and I don't want to be.

I bet, deep down inside, we younger girls and you older girls share some common beliefs. For

instance, we know on a gut level that slut shaming, bullying, and rape culture hurts. However, the
root of all these problems is judgment. Let's not be
terrorized by each other's judgment. Girls are often
turned against each other. We are taught that we
should gossip, get in fights, and pick each other
apart. We're taught to slut each other as a way of
gaining power and status—as a way of putting powerful girls in their place. But I wish we could feel a
sense of community and trust—and I hope you feel
that way when you think of me. My wish is that,
next year, when you look at me you see a little bit of
you and where you've been. Together we can model
something better for the girls who come after us.

Thank you,
Younger Girl

The Text I Can't Delete
Darci, 15

In middle school, having a boyfriend was really
important if you wanted to be socially acceptable.
There was something about having someone want
you that made other people either want you or want
to be you, and it somehow turned into some sort of
vicious circle of want and desire. Kind of intense for
eleven- to fourteen-year-olds right? Well, in eighth
grade, I wanted to be a part of that cycle. There was
something so cool and so mysterious about it—having a boyfriend seemed so adult and grown-up, and
I was completely enthralled by this idea. (Thanks
to every romantic movie or lusty TV show I've ever
seen.) There was this one guy Nick, and I had a crush

on him and I guess he had a crush on me back, and *boom*—we were labeled as a couple, because that's how middle school relationships work.

A week after we started going out, I was sitting across from Nick and his friend Jack in the hall-way—Jack was also a good friend of mine. They were sitting there messing around on Nick's phone, typing and laughing. They saw me watching them, and called out, "Hey! Check your phone." My phone started vibrating and texts flowed in from Nick saying things like, "You slut. You're such a little whore, get the tampon out of your ass, your pussy is probably so tight, you're a fucking slut." I was mortified. What was going on? This was coming from someone I had a crush on, someone I was supposed to be in a relationship with—I was devastated to get this negative attention from him. And, on top of it all, Jack didn't stop Nick from sending the texts! I felt like complete shit. I began questioning everything I'd done over the last week.

What did I do that got me labeled a slut and a whore? I hadn't hooked up with anyone else, I wasn't around that many guys, I usually stayed with my group of close girl friends, and when I wasn't in class or with my friends, I was with him. I was extremely embarrassed to be the target, I didn't want anything to do with him, and I actually started to convince myself that maybe I was a slut. Even though I wasn't sure what actions of mine would've characterized me as one, I started to believe it.

On my way to my class, one of the assistant principals saw I was upset. I broke down and told her what happened. She took me to the higher-ups in the administration and they talked to me about everything. I was kind of in a daze as they took screenshots of the texts and had me write a detailed report. They were clearly as stunned as I was.

When the administration talked to Nick, they admonished him for hurting my feelings, and told him what he said was "inappropriate" for school. He was told to apologize. He never did. But that's not the thing that most upsets me. What infuriates me beyond words is that no one ever told him why calling me a slut and a whore wasn't okay. Do I think Nick felt bad? Yes, but not for the right reasons. He felt bad because he got caught and was required to spend the next day doing community service as his punishment.

Now, I look back on that middle school day as a teaching moment in my life. I think it's unfortunate that the words of one person can make us completely change how we think about ourselves. Over the past year, I've learned the name for what Nick did to me—it's called slut shaming and it's done to take girls down. There is no real definition for the word slut, but in today's society, we've created countless instances where someone's actions can be justified as slutty. Slut shaming affected me because I let words like slut and whore convince me that I was less of a person—which is exactly what those words are meant to do. People think that calling someone slut, whore, ho, THOT, bitch, or any word of similar connotation can be funny or even sometimes affectionate, but it's really a form of bullying and degradation. We shouldn't let labels define us; we define us.

Feminism = Equalism
Max, 16

My friend Nick's ex-girlfriend, Amy, recently complained to me about rumors Nick had started about her. At first I sort of shrugged and had a "what can you do?" attitude. This changed when I realized he was calling her a slut because she hooked up with a guy at a party after Nick broke up with her. This was completely absurd (and blatantly sexist) because he and I were at that same party and we both hooked up with more than two girls each, and we got nothing but praise from our friends. Even Amy was happy for me. Ever since my waking up to the double standard, I started confronting guys, and girls, who call girls sluts for hooking up with someone at a party.

Soon word spread that I was willing to listen to girls and their problems. That was when the first of my friends came to me to talk about rape. I was completely shocked by her confession. The idea that another kid could actually do such a heinous thing to a girl I was friends with was beyond my comprehension. Obviously, it was a much more emotional experience for her and I did my best to be supportive, but it left me very distraught and concerned for the rest of my friends. Then more girls I knew came to me with similar stories. It got to a point where I was beyond my limit. One of the most upsetting parts of the stories I heard was that almost all sexual assaults my friends had endured were committed by guys my own age or slightly older. These guys had absolutely no respect for my friends and most of the time viewed it as normal and acceptable behavior; one even posted on my friend's Facebook wall about what a "good time" he had. I realized simply being sad and consoling my friends wasn't enough. I decided to do something about it.

So I embraced my male feminism. Feminism has many mixed connotations with guys. A lot of us see it as a joke; few of us really have learned what it is. For a long time I viewed modern feminism as pointless: a "women are better than men" movement. Then my friend Samia showed me the truth about feminism. Feminism is an equality movement. Samia even encouraged me to look at it as "equalism." All of the controversy and confusion dropped away when I thought about it that way. Girls are our equals, so shouldn't they be treated as such? The double standards my friends have to deal with and the sexual violence they endure are perfect examples of why feminism matters and sexism needs to go. I mean, the idea that one gender is better (or more entitled) than the other is just idiotic.

Samia also shattered my view of feminists as bra burners (surprising to me, a myth), and showed me that feminists were normal people. For example, she showed me how my mom was, in fact, a feminist: My mom became a doctor at a time when most of her student body was male; she was top of her class; she went to a high school that was originally all boys; my mom kept her name and is, in every way, a proud independent woman. Along with this pretty impressive résumé, she also had me via in vitro fertilization with my dad.

As a guy, announcing my feminism to the world

was impressive to most girls; what girl doesn't like it when a guy treats them like, you know, a person? However, it has not resulted in such a great response from guys. But I don't care. After I educated myself and realized my stance on the issues my friends are dealing with every day, I wanted to change everything. Starting with this: schools across the country should have comprehensive lessons on respect and consent.

I started the petition Just Hear No supporting the teaching of respect and consent in New York City schools. I would hope that most guys would not disrespect women in front of their mother, so that needs to start playing out even when our moms aren't in the room. Fortunately (and I really believe this), most guys are decent and if they actually listen to feminists (their friends and peers) they would feel inclined to support them. At this point, I am fully confident that guys will recognize the damaging effects of the slut shaming double standard and accept "equalism" as only fair and right. I woke up to feminism when given the chance. I want to provide that chance for other guys.

The Sisterhood of the Nightmare Pants
Willa, India, and Soren, 16

WILLA: I remember my freshman-year orientation day. They went over the general rules of the school, including the dress code. They then did a demonstration showing why the dress code should be followed. There was one guy on the stage accompanied by about three girls. I remember clearly that one of the girls dressed in a tank top bent over so her cleavage was on display, and said in a flirty voice, "Hi! Good morning, Mr. Davis!" to the guy (playing "Mr. Davis") who then "acted" all uncomfortable and distracted. This was the way my school decided to demonstrate the impact of not following the dress code. This demonstration was completely absurd. What struck me most was that this girl was supposedly addressing a teacher! What was this demonstration really saying? That girls should be objectified by their teachers? Or girls better cover up or they might get objectified by their teachers—or their teachers might not be able to focus and do their jobs if girls wear tank tops?! It's shocking and hard to believe that girls shouldn't be allowed to wear whatever they want to wear so the faculty won't get distracted. It's also unfair that girls are told to cover up for the boys' sake. The boys, instead, should learn to not be distracted—that's a good life skill, right? Something they'll need out in the world, a world that they share with girls and women, right? It shouldn't be a huge struggle for them to do well in school if a girl shows some skin. Basically, the dress code demonstration at school was saying: a girl shouldn't reveal too much, so the men in the environment, both students and teachers, won't be distracted. And this is what I'm saying: that is completely ridiculous and sexist.

INDIA: Here we are. Sixteen years old and struggling to keep it all together even as the homework keeps piling on, our relationships become more complicated than we could ever imagine, and we feel a new pressure all of a sudden to figure out where we belong. When I imagined becoming a high schooler, these were all things I expected. SATs, ACTs, Subject Tests, APs, you name it, I had imagined the worst. But never did I once imagine that for a teenage girl, the presence of rips in her jeans could be the difference between normalcy and detention, and that her style could be used to shame and objectify her in front of her teachers and peers. Yet this is just what I, what we all, were confronted with against our will.

My freshman year of high school, our dean of students introduced us to a whole new level of public humiliation when she explained the concept of the huge, baggy, blue sweatpants we girls would become quite familiar with as the school year continued. You could spot these sweats from a mile away. The general dress code at our school for bottoms was, and remains to be: skirts and dresses must be as long as the tips of your fingers, when standing up straight. But it became clear that this was a very subjective rule. Some days two girls would wear virtually the same length shorts and only one would be forced to change—the same with dresses, skirts, or ripped jeans.

By chance, or miracle, or whatever you choose to call it, I was never forced to wear the dreaded "dress code-violation sweatpants," but I had several friends who were. One friend explained how she had been called out by one of her teachers for her shorts. She had been swiftly sent to the upper school office, where she was forced to change pants (there were also various oversized shirts available for crop top-wearing bad girls, but these were a bit less humiliating, as well as less common), and spend the rest of the school day in the hideous sweats that screamed, "Hey! I broke our school's dress code today, and therefore I deserve to be publicly shamed!" Not only did this policy embarrass many teenage girls (it is important to note that not a single teenage boy was ever seen sporting punishment pants), it also quickly gave these girls a completely unfair "bad reputation" with the teachers and peers who saw them wearing the sweatpants, bringing on frustrating social and educational repercussions.

All girls have different body shapes and sizes, as well as style. Thanks to the voices of some disapproving parents and students, our dress code policy has improved significantly, and no longer includes the sweatpants of shame. However, it still shocks me how sexist and arbitrary dress codes remain, targeting certain girls because of the way the clothes look or fit on them, and not by one set of standard rules that is fair to both sexes and the student body as a whole. This passive-aggressive slut shaming coming from, of all places, the administration—that we, as young adults attending the school, should feel free to come to with anything for advice or help or trust—is unacceptable. Publicly humiliating young girls because of the way they choose to express themselves is unacceptable, and I hope that it won't be long until everyone, boys, girls, teachers, parents, and students alike all feel the same way about the issue as I do, because it doesn't take a genius to draw a line between the sometimes necessary discipline that occurs in schools (i.e. detention or suspension for violence or serious breaches of academic integrity), and a policy that targets young girls and seeks to alienate them from their teachers and friends in order to prove a sexist point.

SOREN: I remember clearly the feeling of shame I felt the first time I was told by a teacher that my outfit was "inappropriate." I was wearing some weird tribal-print crop top and high-waisted purple jeans. To be honest, my so called "crop top" wasn't all that cropped. When I was sitting normally my shirt barely came above the top of my pants. There was maybe a half a centimeter of skin showing at any given time. The incident happened around 7th period, so naturally I was tired from the school day. All I did was raise my arms above my head to stretch because, as I just mentioned, I was tired. This caused my shirt to come a bit above my belly button (I'm guessing). My teacher immediately came over to me and told me that unless my shirt stayed below the top of my pants for the rest of class, I would be asked to go to the office and put on a giant, sweaty sweatshirt that they make us wear when our clothes are deemed inappropriate (and they don't wash it either). The teacher proceeded to announce that it was a huge distraction to the class. My innocent freshman self was horrified and embarrassed. I couldn't even look at the teacher for the rest of the class.

Now I am a junior. Thinking back, I really don't see how this was a distraction. I mean really, I know freshman boys (and girls too, to be honest) are in the process of learning to control their hormones but I hardly think that is my problem. My stomach cannot be that enticing to them, and if it is, that is their responsibility, not mine. Should I have to put on a big sweatshirt on a hot summer day? What if I'm distracted by the boys' boxers I see every day peeking over their drooped pants? So why isn't that considered a distracting distraction? How about this: I'll put on a sweatshirt when they pull up their pants. And if I can't wear a tank top, why can boys walk around in the incredibly ridiculous-looking tank top that is pretty much identical to the one I'm dressed in?

I have been told multiple times that I was showing too much skin "for a high school girl." What does that even mean? And honestly, what do the staff and teachers of the school expect me to wear on an eighty degree June day? I am not ashamed of wearing a tank top or having my shorts end above my fingertips so why should the administration care? The reasons behind the dress code at our school are completely misguided and even if the code wasn't meant to only apply to girls—girls are the only ones who are affected.

If dress codes are going to continue, I think schools need to come up with real reasons that aren't incredibly sexist, and they need to include boys who are just as much to blame for wearing these "inappropriate" clothes. In conclusion, who gets to decide what is inappropriate and what isn't?

Abercrombie Ass Grab
India, 17

It was freshman year and my first time cutting school. I planned out the whole day with three of my friends and I was beyond excited. I felt so grown-up, you know? Badass and adult. Yeah, I was breaking the rules . . . AND I was doing it in my tight Hollister tank top and my white Abercrombie short shorts that I still love to this day because they make me look five shades darker than I really am. Don't judge me for my brand love. It was 2010. A year when almost everyone in the city had a very public obsession with Abercrombie and Hollister, with their half-naked models greeting people who had actually waited in line to enter their stores. I mean, who didn't want to get in on that? I was standing in the subway, feeling confident, listening to my music on my way to Union Square, holding onto the pole when suddenly, out of nowhere, this middle-aged guy groped me. He just completely went for it and squeezed my ass as if I were just this public thing there for anyone to grab onto—like that pole I was grasping.

I really freaked out. I felt my stomach drop. I was too scared to look up from the ground. I didn't even want to look at him. With my head now down in shame, I shifted so my body was out of his reach and pretended to keep my cool. I was shaking, my hands got so wet and slippery that I could barely hold on any longer, my hand kept falling and I jumped when it touched some random person's hand below mine. I felt him staring at me. I wanted to turn around and scream FUCK YOU, but I was silent—I had been silenced. It was a crowded train and what would everyone think? My shorts were too short and my tank top was too tight. I knew that everyone would think I was a "slutty teenage girl" and I was "asking for it." Why else would I wear that outfit? Was I desperate for attention? Pathetic slutty girl with her ass in everyone's face? I felt myself start to get smaller. I saw my reflection in the subway doors—who was this girl?

Just ten minutes before, I was confident I looked amazing. I felt really good. It wasn't about the brand, it was about the way my body felt and looked. I felt like a model in *Cosmo* or *Elle*, basically half-naked and deserving of everybody's attention and admiration. Powerful. Was that wrong? Was it wrong that I wanted to feel like those girls? The moment before this man grabbed me, I felt good and didn't care about anyone's criticism or judgment. I wanted to feel desired and sexy. Yes, I wanted that. But I didn't want what actually happened to me on that Q train. I didn't want to be touched, and made to feel like a slut who deserved it—I didn't want to be made to feel like I wasn't even a person.

Rachel's Loss
Mandia, 15

I had a friend named Rachel, and I was one of her only friends. A lot of girls didn't like her, you know—I didn't understand why, really, she was pretty and nice. She's Jamaican, like me, but she moved here from Jamaica a couple years ago. You could tell, because she had this cute, really thick accent. Anyway, when she moved here they put her into my sophomore class. She was supposed to be a junior, but they thought she should be placed in a lower grade due to her "language barrier."

So Rachel was in my class and naturally, I heard rumors—I mean, there are rumors out there about everyone—but the things being said about Rachel were terrible. According to the rumor mill Rachel was everything from a professional whore to the school slut. Anything derogatory you can think of, she got stuck with that label. Any promiscuous activity you can imagine, she was supposedly taking part. The crazy thing was even my closest, nicest, and most understanding friends would hear this stuff and believe it! My friends who never had a single conversation with Rachel, never heard her talk about how hard it was being thousand of miles away from home, never saw the way tears welled up in her eyes when she spoke about wanting to make it in America, never noticed how hard she tried not to disappoint her Momma back home—took the gossip as truth. I hated hearing the trash people were talking and soon I got sick of just listening. These people didn't know this girl! They didn't know what she had been through, what she was going through—the girls at my school were vicious.

So months passed by and things got so bad Rachel transferred out of our school. We stayed in touch as best we could—texted each other, always made sure the other was still alive, you know . . . The scary thing was, the gossip kept coming—she'd left and they still couldn't leave that poor girl alone! One day Rachel and I planned to meet up; she came to the football game to hang with me, we wanted to catch up. We hadn't really, officially, sat down and talked since right after she left school. We watched the game together and we were having a really good time! Then, at a certain point, she became sort of quiet, a quiet like she had something on her chest.

Eventually she pulled me to the side, she was like, "Girl, I gotta tell you something, and you can't tell nobody," and I was like, "You know I won't." Slowly, she let it all out. One night, she caved in and had sex with this terrible, notorious guy, Victor, from her neighborhood and now she was pregnant. She swore this wasn't really who she was and begged me not to judge her. She said she wasn't okay and needed support. She told me when she told Victor he said, "Are you sure it's mine?" And she said, "Yes." Then he just turned his back on her, "I don't know what you want me to do. Go, better take care of it." She told me she was feeling lost and really sad, and that the worst part of it all was calling home to Jamaica to tell her mom. Her mother had screamed at her and called her a slut. Rachel cracked a smile, "Girl, I felt like she was gonna reach right through the phone and smack me!" I tried to laugh along with her but the story just got worse.

Rachel was going to all the doctor's appointments by herself, and baby stuff was so expensive and she was struggling—no one was willing to help her. The girls at her new school talked about her growing stomach and called her a whore, slut, pig, you name it. I remember feeling so angry—angry at myself for not being there in those months, angry at the boy (who was 50 percent responsible) for leaving her alone, angry at her family for judging her, and angry at all the girls out there who slut shamed her. It was too much for her—too much for one girl, only sixteen, to deal with.

And then her belly was gone. She wasn't pregnant anymore. When one of the girls from her school got in her face, Rachel tried to defend herself and the girl punched her in the stomach. It was a rough fight, girl-on-girl, and Rachel lost the baby.

She looked at pictures of the sonograms for a while after that. I cry for her all the time. I cry for the way people talked about her, for the way they shamed her, I cry for her baby, I cry for every girl like Rachel. Girls no one cares about enough to listen to their story. Girls who are called sluts. Girls for whom no one shows empathy. I've been called a slut and I know how it feels, eyes on your back with no one really understanding your struggle.

Rachel's story always stays with me, bothers me, angers me—why are we so quick to judge each other? To slut each other? Instead of tearing each other apart, we should struggle through together, using our power and fury to build a world we can thrive in.

Best Friend, No Slut
Prince Akeem, 20

This is a journey through my ego. Before I learned
   not to shame girls I adore.

Jackie always was this pretty young thang and
   kinda after me,
Naw . . . but she used to hang out with me.
Me and the guys.
She was actually my best friend. I know. Surprise!
She was so funny—had everyone crackin.

And I just couldn't resist her beautiful brown skin,
And though she had this brain that always got me
    thinkin,
I always had words for her in my head when I was
    drinkin
and on the inside sinkin:
Ho, bitch, slut, dick rider . . .
'Cause, see, Jackie always got mad attention . . .
From the *other* guys. Did I mention?
And she liked that shit, and man, it filled me with
    this tension.
I felt like I wasn't a man in my circle—unwanted by
    this girl
My longtime friend in this world.

How was I not enough? You feel me?

So, one day I let her know: yo, this is where girls
    stand.
I said straight out: you a THOT, the way you act—
    don't forget I'm the fucking man.

SLAM. She's down. I'm up.

Then a week goes by and I saw her walking down
    the block,
Her head hanging so low she could kiss that block.
Her tears were coming fast as rain
And I knew I had caused that pain.
Damn. Why? Why'd I do that?

Like I was electrified, I jolted awake, and I tried,
One . . .

Me: Jackie I'm sorry!
Jackie: Fuck out my face.
Two . . .
Me: I never meant to hurt you.
Jackie: Really? Well . . . Bye!
Three . . .
Me: Jackie, I deserve everything you throw at me—
   you deserved none of that shit that spewed out
   of me. I was definitely an asshole for power.
   I was fucked up to risk losing my best friend
   because I let jealousy get the best of me. I was
   out of my mind. I was WRONG, you see? You
   matter. I am sorry . . .

Silence.

After all the shit I did, would she give me a pass?
Honestly, what I probably deserved was her size six
   shoe up my ass.

But she hugged me.

I got a hug for owning up to my actions.
And Jackie was bigger than me (and most men)
   with her forgiving reaction.

Fast forward to today—we're good, but it's not the
   same.
And for my failure to treat her with respect and
   love, I'm still ashamed.

Because Jackie and all women deserve to be FREE,
They deserve to get to be who they want to be,

Intellectually, sexually . . .
Without any shut down from you and me.

I'll never say that shit again.

So that's my story and I hope you understand
Shaming another human being (women are human
    beings) doesn't make you a man.

Not All Fun at Funside
Maya, 14

Since I've become a feminist I've started to see
things that never used to faze me in a completely
new light. The commodification of female bodies in
media (and everywhere else), exploitation of female
sexuality, and a lot of other awful stuff that, unfortunately, I have in some way been a part of—as a victim, bystander, or perpetrator—all pop out intensely,
upset me, and make me pissed. The shitty, pertinent,
and most awful winner here is the amount of slut
shaming I have accepted or been a part of. I will
remember something that happened and I'll realize
how not okay it was and I'll feel saddened—especially when it was a pseudo happy, seemingly fine
memory that is now forever fucked. When Katie and
Meg asked me to write this, I went through a mental
list of not-so-great things that I've experienced (sob),
and this one—while not the shittiest—in hindsight
seems so just, like . . . "WHAT? REALLY?"

I'm half Hungarian and my family spends part
of each summer in Hungary. Last summer, when I

was thirteen and going into freshman year, I went to this bilingual Hungarian-English sleepaway camp with the unfortunate name of Funside. Within a day, I had a reputation. I cut my camp T-shirt into a tiny little crop top. I got caught smoking cigarettes with maintenance boys on the first day (ooh rebel). I was this loud, flirtatious, mildly attractive American girl from New York City, and I really played it up (ohmigod). In hindsight, it's all kind of like, "Wow, I was obnoxious. Wow, but I felt so sexy and mature and rebellious. Wow, I didn't realize that in mildly traditional Hungary, wearing my usual belly shirts and not realizing that maybe it wasn't okay to act the same way in Hungary as I did at home was a bit naive, and dialing it up for effect was stupid . . . " I mean, actually it wasn't stupid or naive, because obviously I should have been able to express myself, but I could have been a little bit more aware . . .

There was this clique of guys that my friends and I were hanging out with, and they were kind of into me until . . . I poked my friend's breast, as a joke. I don't know about you guys, but as a bisexual girl with friends who are comfortable with their bodies (although boundaries of all kinds are totally legit) a breast poke normally wouldn't be a big deal at ALL. But all those boys freaked the fuck out. Excessive hooting, vulgar commentary, excessive gossiping about this big "event." My friend, Zsofi, was also like, "Maya, now they think that I'm a slut for letting you do that!" When they "found out" that I'm bisexual it became the hottest topic at camp.

The next night, I was with the boys at the dance

and talking to a counselor who told me, "The guys all told me you touched a girl's breast. You shouldn't tease them like that, it's not fair." This kind of made me sputter, "Um . . . what? . . . erm . . . um . . . nononono." (So I'm a tease?!) The next day the guys were total assholes to me, culminating with me being called "a cheap whore" and a "filthy slut" among some other equally awful and sexually degrading things. This made me cry. I wanted to go home. A few days later, I found out that the boys' counselor had discussed me with the boys—he said I was a tease, and then they all decided I was a slut, whore, etc. They acted as if it is the worst thing in the world: a female being sexual. They acted as if I had committed some terrible sin by being provocative, being curious. As if there is even such a thing as being a tease or a slut.

Those boys who had been interested in me now thought I was trash, worthless, disgusting. They called me a cheap prostitute. The saddest part is that I was so hurt and insulted but all I remember saying is: "If I was a hooker, I would not be cheap!" I hate that that was my only comeback. I hate that I didn't confront them for belittling me and shaming my sexuality. I hate that I still thought they were cute.

I continued to be in touch with one of the boys when I got back to the States and I reread our chat records recently. I came across this lovely nugget: "Wow, you aren't even a slut at all! They were wrong! You're great!" Okay . . . Thanks.

Real
Sabrina, 19

Do you know how it feels
to not be comfortable in your own skin?
Waking up every day and wishing
You looked like somebody else?
Finding beauty in everything
In everyone
Except yourself?
Saying all types of things inside your head
I'm fat
I'm ugly
I'm something no man will ever want or be with.
How could anyone see the beauty in a hideous
    creature like me?
Do you know how it feels?
To see yourself as nothing more than a failure,
Alone in the future
Disappointing friends and family who thought you
    would beat the odds and become something
    AMAZING?
Do you know how it feels?
To fall for the same tricks over and over
Putting yourself in the same position, never
    learning your lesson?
Falling for the same fool who in the end wants
    only one thing
That you continue to give them
Hoping they won't leave
Failing to see
That you deserve better?
Do you know how it feels?

To lose all faith
All hope
Give up on everything 'cause you can no longer
  cope
With the stress
The pain?
You wish the blood would stop rushing through
  your veins
Your heart would stop pumping
And your lungs would stop breathing
You'd wake up
And this would all be a dream, it'd all be a joke
And the past never happened
Then reality kicks in and you realize that this is
  your life
Flashing
Before your eyes.
You can't change what has already happened
It's only the future you can control
And it's up to you to go down the right path
Or choose the same old route
Do you know how it feels to BE ME?
That
I highly doubt.

Define Slut
Marquis, 18

*Slut: A woman who has many sexual partners, a
slovenly woman, a promiscuous woman.*

If you look up the word slut you'll find hundreds
of different definitions. You will however, be hard

pressed to find one that does not include the word "woman" or "girl." These definitions do not encompass both genders. They are not for me or for any man. Knowing this, the word should begin to rear its ugly head. Because what is this word if not plainly, obviously, an attempted attack on all women. What insults are there for me if I am promiscuous? Does promiscuity even exist in a man's world? Does it take any forms other than a pat on the back, a congratulatory exclamation? The word slut perpetuates the idea that anyone should have any say at all in what another person does with his or her own body. At the most fundamental level this is wrong. This is systematic oppression. This is slut culture. A culture that so many young people are steeped in their entire lives. It is poisonous. It chips away at our compassion. It is the reason why the man that catcalls my mother on the street does not see that for exactly what it is: completely unacceptable. The reason why some people may ask first for a description of what a sexual assault victim was wearing, not of the attacker. This is slut culture. This must be done away with.

Why *SLUT*?
Theater as Activism

KATIE CAPPIELLO and MEG McINERNEY

In 2007, we established The Arts Effect All-Girl Theater Company to offer girls a supportive space to come together, train as actors, share their voices, and craft sharp, thought-provoking, feminist theater. Since then we've had the privilege of working with courageous ensembles of young artists and activists throughout the country and across the world, dedicated to exploring the realities of girl/womanhood and raising consciousness about the challenges girls face through theater.

We began developing *SLUT* in January 2012 in New York City through weekly creative sessions with The Arts Effect All-Girl Theater Company. During these sessions, the girls, twenty high school students from New York, New Jersey, Connecticut, and Pennsylvania, talked about the usual: dynamics at school, people they hooked up with at last weekend's parties, friendships on the rocks, pressure from teachers, aggressive boyfriends, and judgmental grandmothers. In the midst of all these conversations, we heard one word again and again: slut. "I mean, she's such a slut." "I felt like a slut." "I was dressed all slutty." "Haha. Oh my god, you're a dirty little slut!" The girls delved into heated discussions about how often and why they used the word slut to describe themselves and others. They determined that the word slut served as *the* barometer of female sexuality—the measurement of female status and self-worth.

Sometimes through tears, members of the group explained (and occasionally reenacted) how they'd been slut shamed by girls, boys, women, and men for anything and everything: flirting with upperclassmen, underclassmen, or . . . *anyone*; "strutting" down the hallway; having large breasts; wearing a push-up bra; not wearing a bra; coming out as lesbian, bisexual, or transgender; being poor; being rich; being black; being Latina; being confident; being curious; kissing someone; liking sex; liking their bodies; posting a picture in a formfitting top; eating a popsicle; donning cutoff shorts; saying "vagina"; buying condoms . . . you name it. What stood out most: the girls revealed they'd been "slutted" after both consensual sexual experiences and experiences of sexual violence. In fact, a third of our girls shared that they'd experienced sexual assault.

What added to their frustration was the reality that the word slut functions simultaneously as a scarlet letter *and* a badge of honor. There's an attempt being made by girls and young women across the country to reclaim the word. Being a "slut" means you're sexy, fun, experimental, experienced, willing, popular, wanted, "fuckable," someone who parties, someone with friends, someone with power . . . and it means, most importantly, that you're not a prude.

As one of our girls said, "The theory is if you can't beat it, own it . . . hey, sex isn't bad, being sexy isn't bad, so 'slut' can't hurt me, right? So I'll show them it doesn't hurt me by using it. The problem is, it can hurt you and it does hurt you. And it's just too hard to walk the line. Eventually you stumble or you get thrown down and any positive connotation disappears. Honestly, I can't think of another word that makes girls feel more degraded and worthless."

In the past few years, slut shaming has been all over the news. Georgetown student Sandra Fluke was called a slut by Rush Limbaugh for her support of women's access to birth control. Steubenville happened. Dominique Strauss-Kahn, the managing director of the International Monetary Fund (IMF), was arrested for sexually assaulting a female hotel-room attendant while visiting our city—she was subsequently attacked and accused of being a "hooker" by the *New York Post*. We watched the girls from New York City's Stuyvesant High School take on the school's slut-shaming dress code. Torrington, Connecticut happened. The tragic suicides of Audrie Pott and Rehtaeh Parsons—teenage girls who had been raped, then slut shamed by their communities—were reported. The devastating impact of slut culture was on full display and it felt more necessary than ever to give voice to those living this reality every day, those we often don't hear from: the girls.

We hunkered down. Team members brought in stories to share and deconstruct. We held workshops and improvised countless variations of conflicts and relationships in hopes of discovering scenarios that best captured the complexity of slut shaming and sexual violence. Through reflective writing, we explored the different perspectives we aimed to incorporate. We and the girls talked to middle school, high school, and college students about their personal experiences as we developed the story line, characters, and dialogue to ensure the piece was authentic, nuanced, and hard-hitting. By January 2013, Katie had completed the script. It's important to note that everything in this play is inspired by real events.

In August of 2013, *SLUT* became an official selection of the New York International Fringe Festival and had its world premiere at the Lynn Redgrave Theater. To date, the girls have performed to sold-out audiences at theaters, museums, courthouses, coffee shops, art galleries, and universities throughout the country.

Our intention in creating and producing *SLUT* is to tell the truth—a truth that #YesAllWomen know too well. Brought to life by real girls, this play exposes the damaging language, shame, and deep-rooted sexism that fuel rape culture. While we don't believe *SLUT* preaches answers, we know it poses necessary questions. By holding a "mirror up to nature" and creating a live communal experience, something you can't turn off, log out of, minimize, or mute, we are determined to artistically ignite serious conversations about the effects of slutting on the lives of young people, the ways we all contribute to this culture, and what we can do to shift the tide.

It's important to remember that experiences of sexual shaming and rape are different for everyone and are largely impacted by gender, race, socioeconomic status, religion, etc. The journey of Joey Del Marco (whom you'll meet in a moment) is the one that we and our students were moved to share. We know many more stories and perspectives need to be brought to light for this conversation to be as rich and far-reaching as necessary to combat these challenges. We look forward to seeing and reading more plays tackling sexism and sexual violence that give voice to those not fully represented in *SLUT*, and supporting any such work.

Finally, we should say that this has not been the easiest process. While it has been rewarding in every way imaginable, we and the girls have experienced criticism, judgment, and anger. People questioned why we would let young girls take on such an intense issue. Is it appropriate to encourage girls to use offensive language and talk so openly about sex and sexuality? Why are you trying to shock people with the title and the dialogue? Is it healthy for a sixteen-year-old girl to portray a rape victim on stage? Valid questions. But, what's there to say beyond this: reputable studies concur that between one in four and one in five women and girls will experience sexual assault.[1] Eighty-one percent of

1. See Finkelhor, D., Hotaling, G., Lewis, I. A., and Smith, C. "Sexual Abuse in a National Survey of Adult Men and Women: Prevalence, Characteristics, and Risk Factors." *Child Abuse & Neglect* 14, no. 1 (1990): 19–28. doi:10.1016/0145-2134(90)90077-7; Krebs, C. P., Lindquist, C. H., Warner, T. D., Fisher, B. S., and Martin, S. L. "College Women's Experiences with Physically Forced, Alcohol- or Other Drug-Enabled, and Drug-Facilitated Sexual Assault Before and Since Entering College." *Journal of American College Health*, 57, no. 6 (2009): 639–49.

kids and teens experience sexual harassment during their middle school or high school years.[2] Clearly, it's time to talk about this, and young people are the ones living it. They are the experts. They have something to say and the stage gives them a place to speak their truths loud and proud, with no censor and no apology. Our girls will tell you, there is power in being part of the solution and they're motivated by a responsibility they feel to stand up for their peers. It's neither girls' nor theater's responsibility to be polite, appropriate, or cute. The goal should be truth, even if the truth makes people uncomfortable.

Inspiringly, for every bit of adversity, we've received an abundance of support. Thank you to the people of all ages from around the world who have courageously come forward with their own stories—vowing to no longer stay silent about their experiences with shame and violence.

We are very proud of the members of The Arts Effect All-Girl Theater Company and the StopSlut Coalition, the powerful activist community that stemmed from this play. Thank you for your bravery, strength, and leadership.

Action is desperately needed, and that begins with awareness and discussion. In our experience, theater provides the most effective platform for shared catharsis, the breaking of silence, and the cultivation of empathy.

2. James E. Gruber and Susan Fineran, "The Impact of Bullying and Sexual Harrassment on Middle and High School Girls," *Violence Against Women* 13, no. 6 (2007): 629.

SLUT

THE PLAY

By Katie Cappiello

Ground Rules for *SLUT: The Play*
(Production and Talkback)

Articulating these ground rules in advance of the play can crucially enhance the experience and reduce anxiety for audience members.

COUNSELORS: This is a dramatic work designed to promote empathy for a silenced but very significant population—people who have experienced sexual violence. By nature, this play can trigger a wide range of emotions, such as sadness, shock, anger, and shame. It's suggested that a professional counselor or therapist (someone who's been trained to talk to people about sexual assault) be available to students and audience members throughout the experience.

TRIGGER WARNING: Prior to the start of the play, a host for the event might consider announcing some version of the following: "This play contains content about sexual assault that may be triggering to some people. Please take care of yourself even if it means exiting the theater." Please underscore verbally that people should leave if they need to—however, leaving in a triggered state involves some risk. People leaving should connect immediately with a safe person or get to a safe place.

SILENCE: *SLUT* has many moments that are quiet, dignified, vulnerable, and intimate. Remind audience members to be respectful—not talking, silencing cell phones, not opening wrappers, and not exiting the room except to take care of themselves.

ALL EMOTIONS WELCOME: Despite the subject matter, this play is not a bummer. It's uplifting. While the topic is serious, there are moments that are hilarious. Feel free to laugh. Your full range of human emotion is invited into this space—it is respected and honored.

SAFE SPACE: After the play, and before talking, assure your participants that this is a safe space. Enlist those participating in the discussion to agree to a level of confidentiality.

S*LUT*, by Katie Cappiello, presented by Evenstar Productions and The Arts Effect, produced by Elizabeth Cuthrell, David Urrutia, Katie Cappiello, and Meg McInerney, coproduced by Jeremy Bloom, production design by Grant McDonald, sound design by Daniel Melnick, lighting design by Gemma Kaneko, production stage manager Jenn Tash, directed by Katie Cappiello and Meg McInerney, had its premiere performance August 19, 2013, at the Lynn Redgrave Theater, NYC, with the following cast:

CAST
(In order of appearance)

JOEY DEL MARCO	Winnifred Bonjean-Alpart
CHRISTINA	Vikki Eugenis
NATALIE	Danielle Edson Cohen
GRACE	Casey Odesser
DANIELLE	Alice Stewart
JANE	Clare Frucht
ANNA	Eliza Price
LEILA	Willa Cuthrell
DOMINIQUE	Amari Rose Leigh
JULIE	Marcela Barry
SYLVIE	Samia Najimy Finnerty

The production was subsequently transferred to the Players Theatre, produced by Elizabeth Cuthrell, David Urrutia, Katie Cappiello, and Meg McInerney, coproduced by Jeremy Bloom, on September 14, 2013.

Pop-up productions, produced by Elizabeth Cuthrell, David Urrutia, Katie Cappiello, and Meg McInerney, coproduced by Jeremy Bloom, were held at the following locations: The Hammer Museum's Billy Wilder Theater in Los Angeles, presented by Equality Now and the Smalley-Wall family, premiered on April 27, 2014; North Dakota State University and Ecce Art Gallery in Fargo, North Dakota, presented by the Feminist Press and Karen Stoker, premiered on May 1, 2014; the Gym at Judson in New York City premiered on May 10, 2014. Technical design for pop-up productions was led by Daniel Melnick with lighting design by Alejandro Fajardo (NYC); stage managers were Janelle Richardson (LA), Laurie Seifert Williams (Fargo), and Niki Armato (NYC). The casts were as follows:

JOEY DEL MARCO	Winnifred Bonjean-Alpart
CHRISTINA	Vikki Eugenis
NATALIE	Danielle Edson Cohen (LA, NYC)
	India Witkin (Fargo)
GRACE	Casey Odesser
DANIELLE	Alice Stewart
JANE	Clare Frucht (LA, NYC)
	Maya Blake (Fargo)
ANNA	Eliza Price
LEILA	Willa Cuthrell (LA, NYC)
	Bella Danieli (Fargo)

DOMINIQUE	Amari Rose Leigh (LA, NYC)
	Darci Siegel (Fargo)
JULIE	Marcela Barry
SYLVIE	Samia Najimy Finnerty (LA, NYC)
	Mary Louise Miller (Fargo)

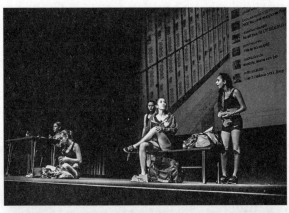

Scenes from the Los Angeles production of
SLUT. Design by Daniel Melnick and Grant
McDonald. Photographs by Barbara Katz.

Characters

JOEY: High school junior, 16.

CHRISTINA: High school junior, 16, member of "the Slut Squad."

NATALIE: High school junior, 16, member of "the Slut Squad."

GRACE: High school sophomore, 15, member of "the Slut Squad."

DANIELLE: High school freshman, 14, new member of "the Slut Squad."

JANE: High school junior, 16, Joey's best friend.

ANNA: High school junior, 16, Joey's close friend, twin sister of Tim.

LEILA: High school freshman, 14, Danielle's best friend, "dating" George.

DOMINIQUE: High school junior, 16, a schoolmate of Joey's, different social circle.

JULIE: High school junior, 17, a schoolmate of Joey's, different social circle.

SYLVIE: High school junior, 16, an acquaintance of Joey's.

Time

Winter, present day.

Place

New York City.

PROLOGUE: PREGAMING

I

SCENE: *The stage is simply set with a screen centered on the back wall. A table and chair are stage right, and a bench or two black boxes are stage left to be used for any of the play's scenes. A water bottle, bottle of vodka, computer, five gym bags, and clothes are set on the stage. An image of a locker room is projected on the screen. It's dark, with only a harsh overhead florescent light shining on* JOEY, *who stands center stage.* JOEY *looks straight out into the audience, sweaty, in shorts and a sports bra. It's dead silent until the other members of the Elliot Dance Team enter.* CHRISTINA, NATALIE, *and* GRACE *burst onto the stage enthusiastically, talking up a storm, dancing around, exhausted from practice.* JOEY *is pulled into the scene. Because she is a freshman,* DANIELLE *stands in the doorway to the locker room, waiting for the upperclassmen to clear out before she's allowed to enter.* NATALIE *looks in the locker-room mirror as she tries to get today's dance sequence just right.* GRACE, CHRISTINA, *and* JOEY *begin to change into sweats.*

CHRISTINA. (*To* NATALIE.) No—no, no, no. Wait. Stop—stop! That's not it. What are you doing? It's this. Okay—it's one-two-three-and-push-and-five-six-kick-seven-and-eight. (CHRISTINA *shows* NATALIE *the dance sequence.*) Yeah. The kick is on the offbeat. (NATALIE *does it again.*) No! (*The* GIRLS *burst into laughter.*) Forget it. Dude, you suck at that shit.

NATALIE. I don't even care. (*She lets out a massive scream.*) I'm so tired! My legs are killing me. What's up with all the squats in warm-up now? PS, did you guys see me trip before my aerial?

CHRISTINA. Yes, and it was amazing. Ms. Miller was just *not* having you today!

NATALIE. I know! . . . I'm a disaster. I'm just so freakin' tired. This week just straight up killed me.

JOEY. Want this? (*She pulls a Red Bull out of her bag, cracks it open, has a sip, and passes it around.*)

NATALIE. Yeah. (GRACE *grabs it before* NATALIE *has a chance.*)

GRACE. (*Takes a sip.*) Ugh—fucking nasty. (NATALIE *grabs it.*)

NATALIE. (*Mockingly.*) Oh my god, Gracie! I'm so sorry we didn't bring any vodka to water it down for ya!

GRACE. (*Mockingly back.*) Oh my god, Natalie, you're just so hilar!

CHRISTINA. Okay, what's everyone wearing to Connor's?

JOEY. I don't know.

GRACE. Lace tank top from Urban, red velvet skirt, don't know what shoes.

NATALIE. My miniskirt thing that's made out of sweater material, no tights, with my mom's Dolce Vita little black booties.

CHRISTINA. Don't call them booties, it sounds weird.

JOEY. Oh! So agree! Like panties—panties and booties are so, like, dainty and, like . . . uh—

CHRISTINA. Victorian, or puritanical, or something.

JOEY. Yes! They sound oddly, like, perverted to me.

NATALIE. Okay. Wow. My mom's Dolce Vita *ankle boots*. How's that for ya? Oh, JoJo, I wanted to ask you, can I borrow your AP World History notes please?

JOEY. Definitely. Here. (*She tosses the notebook to* NATALIE.) You wanna study on Sunday?

NATALIE. Yes please! Hey, do you think your parents will care if we do your house and then your dad can make us pizza? I'm going to carb my ass off.

GRACE. Ugh!! (*She's been examining her upper-inner thigh.*)

NATALIE. What?

GRACE. Fuck!

CHRISTINA. What?

GRACE. Look at this shit. (*She shows everyone her inner thigh.*)

JOEY. Oooff—looks like you got a little chub rub going on there, Gracie.

GRACE. What? I do not. But seriously, what is it? It's like a rash-type thing.

DANIELLE. It's definitely chub rub.

GRACE. (*Kind of jokingly.*) Dude! Dani, why the fuck are you talking? Keep your freshman mouth closed.

NATALIE. It's chub rub.

GRACE. But I'm, like, not fat, am I? And I've never had it before. Wouldn't I have had it before? How is this possible?

NATALIE. Your sexy thighs were smacking against each other during laps or something.

GRACE. It hurts . . .

JOEY. No kidding! You gotta slather Vaseline all over your inner thighs next practice.

GRACE. Does it look that bad? Does it look like it's a cluster of sores or something? Does it look like I have the herps?

NATALIE. Yup. Definitely. Looks just like herpes.

JOEY. You would know.

NATALIE. Thanks!

JOEY. Anytime!

CHRISTINA. (*To* GRACE.) Wow, no one is gonna hook up with you again.

JOEY. Like, ever again. This is a sad day for you, Gracie.

NATALIE. You and George tonight—not happening now, no matter how hot he thinks you are.

GRACE. First of all, I've moved on from George, thank you; and you would know that if you had actually listened to me in chem today. He's hooking up with Annoyingly Cute Freshman Girl. So fuck you, Nat. Second of all, I'm just gonna say two words: Bloody Beaver.

NATALIE. What?

GRACE. Yeah. I'm gonna be the next fucking *Bloody Beaver.*

JOEY. Oh my god, Grace! (*To* NATALIE.) Bloody Beaver. You don't remember that? Hunter Gaynes got everyone calling Nadia Boyd that after they hooked up.

CHRISTINA. Right, right, yes! Yes, okay, but, like, how dumb is she, though? You don't let a guy hook up with you when you have your period. Is she retarded?

JOEY. Don't.

CHRISTINA. Sorry. Is she mentally challenged? God. Anyway, this is not a Bloody Beaver situation Gracie, okay?

JOEY. Yeah, it's definitely not. But for the record, Hunter is a little freshman douche. He put that shit all over Facebook. Fuck him, man. She's like—how even old is she, Dani?

DANIELLE. She's fourteen, but she was thirteen at the time.

JOEY. And it was the first time she ever really hooked up. I mean, she didn't know what to do.

NATALIE. And she's so cute. I love her.

JOEY. Oh, love her.

NATALIE. And she, like, loves us. We should tell all the freshman girls not to hook up with him. Seriously.

JOEY. Yes.

NATALIE. Danielle, tell them. (DANIELLE *gestures in agreement and smiles.*)

GRACE. Hey, hey, hey—what if I wear tights? The ones with the seam up the back so they still look really cute.

NATALIE. Well, considering your drunken strip-tease last weekend, you'll probably end up taking them off anyway, so—

GRACE. Whatever Nat. Jealous? Of my *sex-ay* moves?

NATALIE. Oh, yeah. I'm jealous of *you*, with your chub rub, for sure. Hate to say it Gracie, but that's it for you dude. Sorry. You're a herpes-ridden dirty slut now so—

GRACE. I'm gonna kill you, Natalie. And you should just shut it because you are the biggest . . . dirtiest . . . sluttiest slut of, like, all time. (GRACE *laughs—the following banter is routine for these girls.*)

NATALIE. Hell yeah, I am. Jealous?

JOEY. Okay, no way is she the biggest slut of the Slut Squad! I can slut it up with the sluttiest of y'all, thank you very much! Including Natalie.

CHRISTINA. Hey!

NATALIE. Ohhhh Chrissy! You know we respect your sexy slutness. (NATALIE *digs though her makeup bag.*)

CHRISTINA. You better. And don't make me challenge you to a slut-off.

NATALIE. (*To* GRACE.) Okay, let me see it again. Here. (NATALIE *begins to cover* GRACE'S *rash with concealer and powder.*)

CHRISTINA. 'Cause you'll go down bitches. 'Cause I'll just walk right up to Derek Walker and—

NATALIE. (*Referring to* GRACE'S *crotch.*) Okay, check it out! Look. It's not that bad now, right? I just covered it with concealer and powder. Look.

GRACE. Is it okay? (*They all look at* GRACE'S *thigh.*) Is it crusty? It's totally crusty, right? I'm gonna have a fucking crusty crotch at this party!

JOEY. Grace, it's fine. We're messing with you. Any guy of your choosing will still wanna get all up on your shit and no one is gonna say anything.

GRACE. Okay.

JOEY. And you wanna know why?

GRACE. 'Cause I'm a sexy mama and you love me?

NATALIE. Yep. *And* you don't mess with Slut Squad girls. Because we will take you down, motherfucker.

CHRISTINA. Awww, Slut Squad love!

GRACE. Slut Squad crazy love!

NATALIE. (*Chugs the last of the Red Bull and jumps up on the locker-room bench.*) Slut Squad crazy, mad, stupid love! (*The girls break into their chant, the team anthem. It's goofy and fun, but they kind of mean it . . .*) S-L-U-T S-Q-U-A-D!

ALL.
YES, THAT'S WHO WE BE.

NATALIE.
SAY WHAT?

ALL.
YES, THAT'S WHO WE BE.
AND, BITCHES, WE GO DOWN LIKE NO OTHER
GIRLS IN TOWN. AND WHEN WE STRUT
THROUGH THE SCHOOL,
YOU KNOW WE MAKE THEM BOYS DROOL.
BECAUSE THEY ALL WANNA PIECE OF THIS.
AND YOU KNOW YOU CAN'T SLUT LIKE THIS.
HIS ANACONDA DON'T WANT NONE
BECAUSE YOU AIN'T ME, SON! OH YES.
OUR MILKSHAKE BRINGS ALL THE BOYS TO
THE YARD.
AND THEY'RE, LIKE, IT'S BETTER THAN YOURS.
DAMN RIGHT! IT'S BETTER THAN YOURS.
COULD WE TEACH YOU? HELL NO!

(CHRISTINA, NATALIE, and GRACE exit with all
their stuff, joking, dancing, having fun. DANIELLE
enters and crosses, trying not to get in JOEY's way,
and exits to the showers. Lights fade to black.)

II

SCENE: Music is playing as JOEY gets ready for the
party. She checks herself in the mirror and digs
through her clothes while dancing around. She
is alerted to a video chat coming through on the
computer. She rushes to turn down the music and
answer the call. Her best friend JANE pops up as
a video on the projection screen.

JOEY. Hey!

JANE. Hey!

JOEY. Do you like this lipstick?

JANE. Yeah.

JOEY. How was track?

JANE. Well apparently, I'm slow now, which is frustrating.

JOEY. Oh! Okay, so Gracie has a rash near her crotch. So, the door is open for you with George tonight!

JANE. Oh please, and what? Be, like, the hundredth girl he's hooked up with this year? He's hot, but I don't wanna be one of his, like, bevy of sluts. And isn't he hooking up with Annoyingly Cute Freshman Girl?

JOEY. Yeah, but whatever. (JOEY *continues to dress for the party.*) You're going to come to Luke's with me right?

JANE. I can't. My mom is making me eat here.

JOEY. You know your mom's just banning you from going because Linda's a Republican.

JANE. (*Laughing.*) Yeah probably! She fucking hates Linda. That's why she didn't want me going out with Luke, remember? She was all like, "Janey, hey, if you wanna go out with some kid whose mother thinks it's still nineteen-fucking-fifty, go right ahead. But I'm just warning you, if you get pregnant that woman will be your worst fucking nightmare."

JOEY. (*Laughing.*) Your mom's hilarious.

JANE. Yeah. Who's going to Luke's?

JOEY. (*Putting on shoes.*) Luke, George, me, Anna . . . (*teasingly*) and Tim.

JANE. Shut up. Do you think Anna hates me because I want to hook up with her brother?

JOEY. No.

JANE. I like Tim. He's the only one of those three that's not a dick.

JOEY. Oh, come on! That's not true. George is not a dick. And Luke is just an idiot. (*She is now fully dressed.*) Okay. What do you think? (*Shows her outfit to* JANE.) Too slutty?

JANE. No, it's perfect.

JOEY. I love you. Hey, you wanna sleep over tonight?

JANE. Yeah!

JOEY. My parents will be so excited. They seriously think we're still twelve when we have sleepovers.

JANE. Ha! Funny. Okay, dinnertime. See you later. Love you. Bye.

JOEY. K. Love you. Bye.

(*Screen goes dark.* JOEY *turns the music back on and begins to work on her hair. Again, her video chat begins to ring. She pauses the music and answers.* ANNA *pops up as video on the projection screen.*)

JOEY. Hola!

ANNA. Hey! I can't really talk, but I wanted to video chat you for a quick sec. I'm grounded and they took my phone. I'm sure they're gonna take my computer, too, but I wanted to tell you that I can't come tonight, okay?

JOEY. No! Are you serious? What did you do?

ANNA. Thea was driving me crazy. She wore my sweater to school today and got shit on it. And then she was being all up in my shit from the minute I got home. So I just smashed her in the face. (*They laugh.*) And she, like, threw a shit-fit and my parents went off the deep end at me. So I'm grounded . . . which is really annoying because she totally deserved it, and honestly, I can kinda tell my mom thinks so, too, because she said I can still watch TV.

JOEY. Sucks. I'm gonna murder Thea.

ANNA. Right? She's such a stupid little whore. She's becoming a real bitch, too.

JOEY. She's eleven!

ANNA. (*Hearing her mom coming up the stairs.*) Hey, I really gotta go, but I won't have my phone FYI so . . . or probably this computer so . . . have fun. I'm so jealous! I hate myself right now. Okay, bye.

JOEY. Wait!

ANNA. What?

JOEY. Tim's still coming right?

ANNA. Yeah, yeah. He told me to tell you. He's the current "good child" of the family. Thea and I are fuckups but Timmy's perfect. Have so much fun. Take care of my brother. Keep him away from the ratchet hos, please!

JOEY. (*Laughing.*) Yes! Okay, bye. Love you. Go read something.

ANNA. No way. *Friday Night Lights* marathon.

JOEY. OOOOooo. Tim Riggins!

ANNA. My dream man. I wanna do him.

JOEY. Ha! Love you. Bye.

ANNA. Love you. Bye.

(*Screen goes dark. JOEY turns on the music. She looks at herself in the mirror, satisfied. The music changes, she begins to dance. Lights dim and a spotlight focuses on JOEY as images (photos/video) of the action are projected on the screen. First are images of JOEY pregaming at LUKE'S house, having fun, laughing. Onstage JOEY sings along to the song and drinks vodka from the bottle; she appears to be getting drunk. The projections and music segue into the sights and sounds of a busy New York street. Onstage JOEY is freezing, shaking to keep warm, clearly tipsy, while looking for a taxi. She rushes across the stage, flagging down a taxi.*)

JOEY. You guys, I got one. Let's go. Someone's gotta sit in the front. No, seriously, we're not gonna fit. Someone should sit in the front next to, um, him, um—what's your name, sir? . . . Apunda! Someone's gotta sit next to my friend Apunda up front, okay? Fine. We'll just squish—get in—I'm freezing! Apunda, we're going to Park and 89th.

(*Sound of taxi door slamming shut. The music suddenly stops and the screen goes dark. The same harsh overhead light from the opening of* the play shines on JOEY. *She stands there, dead silent, trying to catch her breath. She turns and violently vomits. Lights slowly come up. Muffled music plays from the other room. Photos of the party are projected on the screen. JOEY is in the bathroom; she sinks to the floor. After a moment, she turns to vomit again. She wipes her mouth and tries to breathe. She takes her cell phone out of her bag. There's a knock on the bathroom door.)*

JANE. *(Offstage.)* Jo, are you okay? *(Another knock.)* Joey, let me in, okay? Come on, it's me. Open the fucking door. Are you okay? *(JOEY gets up and shakily opens the door. The music volume increases for a moment as the door opens. JOEY sits down near the door. JANE enters and locks the door behind her.)*

JANE. Dude, are you okay? You look like shit. Did you throw up? *(JOEY nods her head yes—and suddenly turns and vomits again. JANE rushes to hold her hair back.)* Are you okay? Are you just really fucked up?

JOEY. *(Barely able to talk.)* I'm such a slut. *(She tries to breathe.)*

(Music fades and lights dim. Spotlight on JOEY and JANE as JOEY begins to remove her makeup and JANE helps her into sweatpants and a zip-up sweatshirt. The spotlight fades to black.)

SCENE 1. WHERE DO I START?

SCENE: *Lights up on* JOEY, *sitting at a table downstage right. The rest of the stage is dark. She is being interviewed by the Assistant District Attorney.*

JOEY. You're going to record what I say? . . . Okay . . . should I just start or—Okay. Um, Joanna Grace Del Marco. I'm sixteen years old. I live at 535 East 14th Street, apartment 8F, 10009. That's in Stuyvesant Town . . . What? Oh, okay. Yes, sure, okay. Yeah, I understand, okay. I am agreeing to give this statement without my parents present. Is that what you mean? Okay. (*Beat.*) You can call me Joey, yeah. That's fine. That's, like, what everyone calls me anyway. No one really calls me Joanna except, like, my grandma. (*Beat.*) So . . . Joey's good. (*Beat.*) My mom's still here, right? No, I'm fine. I don't need her to come in. I'm okay. I actually don't want to talk about all this stuff in front of her again right now. Or my dad. That was almost worse than the actual thing, you know, in a way . . . you know, having to tell my dad? I mean, not really. Obviously it wasn't *as bad* but . . . it's awkward now that I know he knows, 'cause he can probably, like, picture it. Which is like . . . I'm sorry, I actually don't feel that good. Could I have some water? Would that be okay? If it's too much trouble, that's totally fine, I just . . . No, I don't need my mom or anything. That's okay. (*Acknowledging the water, she takes a sip.*) Thanks. (*She takes a sip.*) I'm sure I'll feel better after I have a little of this. I just started feeling a little shaky. I'm okay. I'm so sorry. Um . . . okay . . . so, should I just start from the beginning? Okay.

(*Lights up on* JANE *standing stage left in a sweatshirt and jeans. She is in her kitchen talking to her mom.* JOEY *continues making her statement. The dialogue intertwines.*)

JANE. She just went to a party, like we all go to parties . . .

JOEY. Basically, the whole school was there.

JANE. Including me.

JOEY. My mom was comfortable with me going, because I was going with a few of my friends.

JANE. I *always* call you . . . but so does she. She always calls her mom . . .

JOEY. I told her I would call her when I got there and call her again when I left, and that I would take a cab home. That's our, like, usual deal when I want to go out. She calls it the Triple C: Call, Call, Cab.

JANE. What happened in that cab, Mom . . . (*Beat.*) She got in the cab with them because they are her friends. That's so crazy. They're our friends . . .

JOEY. Excuse me? Uh, yes. I would consider Luke a close friend, yes. Luke's mom and my mom have been friends for a long time because they were copresidents of the PTA in second grade. My mom thinks his mom's a little crazy, but our families are friends. I go to his house all the time.

JANE. I can't sleep . . . I barely slept last night. It's just . . . she wasn't supposed to be the only girl at his house. I was supposed to be there, and so was Anna. But Anna got grounded and you wouldn't let me go . . . If you had let me go she wouldn't have been alone. I just feel like some of this is on me . . . What?

JOEY. Because I wanted to. My parents were okay with it and I guess I thought it would be fun. It *was* fun at first, you know?

JANE. She said they were playing video games, they were dancing, they were. . . I *know* they were playing video games because she texted me her high score on Mario Kart while she was there . . .

JOEY. George brought the vodka. Uh, I'm not sure. I think his older brother got it for him.

JANE. I pregame, Mom. I'm sorry. I know you don't want to hear that, but . . . everyone pregames.

JOEY. I had some, yes.

JANE. Who told you she was sloppy drunk?

JOEY. I had two drinks . . . about two. And I know now that that was really stupid. I mean, obviously I wish I hadn't had any.

JANE. I don't understand . . . Okay . . . yeah, I saw them, too. But what is it that you think those pictures show, Mom? Have you seen *my* Instagram lately? She was just messing around. She wasn't sloppy drunk.

JOEY. I actually have, like, pretty little interest in drinking. I'm sure that sounds like a lie or, like, I'm trying to gloss over who I really am or whatever, but it's true . . . It's just sort of hard in certain moments to not do it. I know that's cliché but . . .

JANE. You talked to her about this? But you hate Linda. She sucks. You know she's just talking all this shit because her idiot douchebag son is involved. I mean, *where was she* when all this was going on? Out at dinner! So how would she even know? (*Beat.*) I don't care what the PTA moms think . . .

JOEY. Yes, I've been drunk before.

JANE. Yes, I know.

JOEY. And truth is, I wasn't drunk-drunk. I know what I feel like when I'm really drunk and I wasn't wasted. I just wouldn't be wasted after two or three, like, swigs of vodka. And, I'm not saying drinking is okay . . .

JANE. Yeah, I think in this particular situation, maybe that was a little stupid of her, Mom, yeah . . .

JOEY. It was stupid of me . . .

JANE. But you're not being realistic. I can't think of a single one of my friends who wouldn't have had a drink—

JOEY. I just can't believe this. I mean it's just . . . it was irresponsible of me to drink, I know, but I *was* trying to limit myself, you know. I was *trying* to be careful.

JANE. I feel like you're a different person right now. You've known Joey forever. She sleeps over here or I sleep over there, like, every week since we were nine! And you're acting like—you're acting like you don't believe her. I mean, you believe her, Mom, right? . . . Wait! . . . Are you kidding? What do you mean she exaggerates? What? When, when has she lied? (*Beat.*) That. Was. Eighth. Grade. So she told me she wasn't going to go to a party, and then she went, and I was upset because I felt left out. Whatever, Mom. I'm over it! You should get over it, too. Wow. This is really insane. You don't believe her . . . What the fuck? (*Beat.*) What, you're gonna ground me? Who cares! Do you think I give a crap, Mom? You know, it's really fucked because the funny thing is, we'd probably all be safer if we were all just grounded all the friggin' time, right?

JOEY. I wanted to party, I mean, I guess that's true. So . . . people think I'm a liar . . .

JANE. I can't believe you right now. You know what's so pathetic, Mom? No! I'm not going to stop! You always pride yourself on being this, like, big, like, feminist. You did that fundraiser downtown that time for women in India and wherever else, and you're always saying it's so messed up when people don't take women and girls seriously. And now *you're* not taking Joey seriously. You just called her a liar. You know, you said I could always come to you . . . but now I don't believe you . . . Because . . . What if that had been me? (*She starts to exit, but comes back.*)

JOEY. Stupid me, right? (*Sighs.*) I'm just so mad at myself for trusting them . . . and, like . . .

JANE. I heard you last night, Mom. (*Beat.*) You called her a slut 'cause of what happened. Yes, you did. You called her a "little slut" to Dad when you guys were in the kitchen. I heard you. (*Beat.*) If that had been me, Mom, and I had come to you . . . would you and Dad have called me a slut while making dinner when you thought I couldn't hear? Would the other moms be calling each other talking about what a slut I am, and what a liar I am, and what a sloppy, fucked-up drunk I was? (JANE *exits. Lights dim stage left.*)

JOEY. I just didn't think it would be like this. (*She drinks more water.*) Yeah, I'm fine. I'm sorry. (*Beat.*) Sorry? . . . Oh, uh, I don't know how much they had. I just don't remember. Um . . . I *do* know that we finished the bottle. I know that. Does that help? No, no one was high . . . I mean, does that even matter? I mean, does it matter if they smoke weed sometimes? Do I really have to answer that? Because they didn't have any that night so . . . No, I didn't feel like I needed to call my mom at that point. I had already called her when I got there. And honestly, things were normal. It was not the first time I drank with those guys. We drink together. I know we shouldn't, but we do. I wasn't uncomfortable or scared or anything. I was just hanging out with my friends . . . Right, he lives in the West Village . . . Sure. Tim Delaney, George Wright, and Luke Friedman . . . Uh, yes. Yes, I felt safe with them . . . Well, um, I guess I would say my relationship with them is pretty typical . . .

SCENE 2: GAME OF THRONES

SCENE: *Lights come up on* LEILA *and* DANIELLE, *stage left, sitting with their computers in* LEILA'S *room. They are eating a big bag of Twizzlers while scanning through Ask.fm.* JOEY *continues with her statement; the stories intertwine.*

LEILA. It's just so stereotypical to me, you know?

JOEY. They're my friends . . .

LEILA. They're her "friends."

JOEY. I've known them forever.

LEILA. Who she's known for, like, ever.

JOEY. We hang out every weekend, pretty much.

LEILA. They hang out every fucking weekend. Or better yet, she follows them around every weekend. You know it's true. Wherever George, Luke, and Tim go, she's there.

DANIELLE. I know.

JOEY. I know people maybe think I'm more than friends with these guys because we've, like, minimally made out before but—

DANIELLE. And what? She wants us to believe she's not secretly, or even obviously, into them? Please! Like she's *never* hooked up with any of them?

JOEY. I've never hooked up with any of them.

LEILA. Exactly. Whenever I ask George if they ever hooked up he's like, "Don't worry about it."

JOEY. We all know we're just friends, and we're cool like that.

DANIELLE. And it's so obvious what he means by that . . .

LEILA. Right. He means, "Yeah we've hooked up, but it was nothing. So don't let it get to you." And I don't. I actually don't totally care if they hooked up last year or whatever, but—

DANIELLE. Right.

LEILA. But Friday night—

DANIELLE. I know.

JOEY. Friday night—

LEILA. You don't do that.

JOEY. Was a pretty regular night, except I was the only girl.

LEILA. You don't do that shit with someone else's boyfriend.

DANIELLE. Oh.

LEILA. What?

DANIELLE. Is he really your boyfriend, though?

JOEY. Wait. (*Beat.*) I guess that's not totally the truth.

LEILA. What do you mean?

DANIELLE. Is he technically your boyfriend? I thought you guys were just hooking up.

JOEY. George was actually my first boyfriend.

LEILA. I don't get what you mean by that.

JOEY. He was my fourth-grade boyfriend, which is funny to think about. So, at one point we were more than just friends.

DANIELLE. I have just never heard anyone say he's your boyfriend, including you. And now all of a sudden he's, like, your boyfriend.

LEILA. We talk every day, we went to the movies once, we go to parties together—what do you think we are?

DANIELLE. Okay. Sorry. Maybe that's what you should ask on there. Make some comparison between you and her and see what he says.

JOEY. He was really different then. He carried a *Looney Tunes* lunch box to school. Sort of as a joke. And he had, like, Dennis the Menace hair. (*Beat.*)

LEILA. We haven't had sex.

JOEY. We held hands.

DANIELLE. Okay. Well, I didn't think—

JOEY. That was the extent of the physical contact.

LEILA. Do you think that's a big deal?

JOEY. It was such a big deal at the time, you know?

LEILA. I mean, we've hooked up a little bit but . . . only a little bit . . .

JOEY. I mean we all, like, whatever, with each other. It's nothing. It's just what you do.

DANIELLE. Okay. Well, what do you mean by a little bit? Like next to nothing?

LEILA. I don't know . . .

DANIELLE. You don't know what?

LEILA. Do you think that's why he's technically not my boyfriend?

DANIELLE. I don't know.

JOEY. Yes. Well, I don't know if she's his girlfriend, but George has been hanging out with this girl Leila lately.

DANIELLE. I think he's not technically your boyfriend because he's a junior and you're a freshman and, like, I don't know . . .

JOEY. She's a freshman.

LEILA. I fucking hate Joey Del Marco.

JOEY. She's actually pretty sweet and she's really pretty.

LEILA. I mean, I'm not ready to have sex with him, so she just makes herself available?

JOEY. I sort of feel bad for her because it seems like he's not really, totally into her.

DANIELLE. Yeah. That sucks.

JOEY. No, she wasn't at the party.

LEILA. Like, why weren't we invited to the party?

DANIELLE. Because we're freshman.

JOEY. There were no freshman allowed at the party.

LEILA. God, find your own guy, you stupid whore.

DANIELLE. I think she feels like those are her guys.

JOEY. But, anyway, most of the time George, Luke, and Tim just treated me like one of the guys. (*She takes a sip of water.*)

LEILA. Did she say that?

DANIELLE. No. Not to me but—

LEILA. So I'm just this freshman bitch to her who's taking over her territory?

DANIELLE. I don't know. And stop yelling at me. I'm just saying that's probably how she feels.

LEILA. Whatever. I don't understand why he won't call me or even just text me. I know he's around. What the FUCK?

JOEY. You know, I just don't understand how it got out of hand, you know? It's like, "What?"

DANIELLE. What are you gonna say?

LEILA. I'm gonna just, like, be there for him or whatever, and be, like, "Hey, I got your back."

DANIELLE. Why?

LEILA. What do you mean?

DANIELLE. Well, I just don't know why you'd say that exactly . . .

LEILA. Because I feel bad for him. Are you kidding me? This whole thing is a real shit show. This type of shit can ruin someone's whole life, and I feel bad for him. Because, you know, it's been his dream to go to Harvard like his dad. And his brother went there, too, and his grandfather and stuff, and this could 100 percent ruin that for him. He has got a 4.0 and his SAT scores were ridiculous and he's going to be scouted, or whatever you call it, for crew. It's just messed up . . .

JOEY. This whole thing is so messed up . . .

DANIELLE. Yeah, all of this is really messed up. But why are you getting his back?

JOEY. Back of a cab. They're telling everyone I hooked up with *all* of them in the back of that cab.

LEILA. Because I really like him and I know he didn't mean anything by it. They were wasted. Whatever—it happened. She's a slut, and she was all over his shit. Did you see those pictures? She was basically giving him a lap dance. What was he supposed to do?

DANIELLE. Leila, no matter what happened, right, no matter what actually happened, he still did it. And he's telling people that.

JOEY. They're telling everyone that . . . you know . . .

DANIELLE. You know what I'm saying? He's telling people he hooked up with her. He, like, admittedly messed around with someone else. And you're okay with that? (*Beat.*) You're still gonna hang out with this guy? I mean, what will your parents think? (*Beat.*)

LEILA. Do Joey and the Slut Squad talk shit about me at practice?

DANIELLE. No.

LEILA. Yeah, right.

DANIELLE. Dude, they don't. The only thing I've ever heard them say about you is that you're annoyingly pretty.

LEILA. See? They're out to put me in my place.

DANIELLE. I don't think they are but, okay. Honestly, Leila, I've never heard them say anything bad about you in the locker room or at practice. I would tell you. Why would I cover for them?

LEILA. Why is this happening to me?

JOEY. Why is this happening to me? I keep thinking that, you know? 'Cause we're not like this.

LEILA. I'm not even like this.

JOEY. This is not who we are. We're just not like this, you know?

LEILA. I'm not even into all this shit or whatever. You know I'm not . . .

JOEY. We're all like normal kids, you know?

LEILA. I mean, I don't want to be sitting here stressing about this shit.

DANIELLE. I know.

LEILA. I'd rather be in bed reading, like, I don't know, reading every *Game of Thrones* book all over again and—

DANIELLE. So why don't you? (LEILA *just gives her a look and goes back to her Twizzlers.*) Fine, so just keep hanging out with King Joffrey then!

LEILA. Stop. I am not Sansa!

DANIELLE. You are *so* Sansa . . . sorry.

LEILA. I'm Arya!

DANIELLE. No! You *want* to be Arya but—

(*Suddenly* LEILA *notices something on the computer. The latest Ask.fm post is projected on the screen.*)

LEILA. He answered one!

DANIELLE. Let me see. Move. (*They hover over the computer.*)

JOEY. I mean, you can see that, can't you? It's not who we are. (*She takes a sip.*)

LEILA. Someone was like, "What are you gonna say to Joey when you see her? Or are you never gonna talk to that nasty bitch again?" Okay, I love whoever asked that. So he wrote, "Yeah, we're definitely done with her. She's not a bitch, but we get it. She obviously regrets what she did Friday night, so she feels like she's gotta make shit up."

DANIELLE. Stupid.

LEILA. I'm gonna do it. I'm gonna write something. Hold on. (*She thinks.*) Okay. (*She types and Danielle reads over her shoulder. Her question is projected on the screen.*)

DANIELLE. "Do you think Joey was jealous of your relationship with Leila Zimmer and that's why she threw herself at you? Have you talked to Leila?"

LEILA. Good?

JOEY. I don't know, man . . .

DANIELLE. Yeah. It's good. Let's see what he says. (*They eat more Twizzlers in silence.*)

LEILA. Why is the sex in *Game of Thrones* always doggy style?

DANIELLE. No idea.

LEILA. Is that the only way they do it in Westeros? I mean—

DANIELLE. I know, right?

LEILA. I just . . . really like him.

DANIELLE. I know.

LEILA. "Winter is coming."

DANIELLE. Yup.

(*Lights dim on* DANIELLE *and* LEILA.)

JOEY. I just really liked them. That's the thing. Not like *that*, I swear to god. I just mean as friends. And yeah whatever. I'll just say it . . . I liked the attention. I'd be lying if I said I didn't. It's fun to have that attention, you know? I mean, all girls feel that way . . . and I mean any girl who says she doesn't is lying. I'm sorry. I love girls who say that, you know? Because they're lying. They're not above it, you know? They're just not. So . . . (*Beat.*) Do we really need to talk about that again? I just . . . Yes, CVS. Yeah. I had stopped there on the way to Luke's to get some deodorant. I was worried I smelled bad, okay? And then I was like, "Well, I haven't eaten all day really, so I need something to fill me up so I won't get sick if I drink" . . . So I got some Twizzlers and . . . No I'm okay. I'm just feeling really, like, frustrated with all this . . . Because it was just a stupid thing I did. I mean, haven't you ever done a stupid thing? I just don't get how this means that I . . . I mean, do you think they'll say that? Do you think that's what they're gonna say I was trying to do? . . . This is just so unbelievable!—Sorry. I'm sorry. I'm being really . . . rude to you, I feel like . . . No, I am. I'm sorry. I just sort of . . . hate . . . myself, but whatever. (*Building herself up a little . . .*) Let's just do this.

SCENE 3: JOEY BLOW ME

SCENE: *Lights come up stage left as* DOMINIQUE *and* JULIE *enter. They are roaming the aisles of the CVS, loitering in the cosmetics section. The condom aisle is projected on the screen.* DOMINIQUE *is texting.* JULIE, *looking at lip glosses, appears impatient.* JOEY *continues with her statement; the stories intertwine.*

JULIE. Let's just do this already.

DOMINIQUE. Hold on. (*She reads a text out loud.*) "Dominique ur magnifique." He's so the cutest, though, right? (*She continues to text.*)

JULIE. Dylan? Um, yes.

JOEY. Yes. I did it.

JULIE. Why don't you just ask him to do it?

DOMINIQUE. No. Are you stupid?

JOEY. And it was stupid, I guess. Another example of me being a stereotypical stupid girl that night.

DOMINIQUE. I'm not asking him to buy condoms.

JULIE. Why?

DOMINIQUE. Because then he'll think I want to have sex.

JOEY. I bought condoms and I brought them to Luke's. But that doesn't mean I wanted to have sex.

JULIE. But you do.

DOMINIQUE. Yeah, but I just don't want him to know that I want it, you know? It's too . . . odd. I just want to have some in my bag in case things start to happen. He, like, never has one. He just can't get it together, you know? So then this time we won't have to stop because *I'll* have one. And we won't go through that weird, unnecessarily awkward moment of, like, "Oh, let's just dry hump then . . . again."

JULIE. Okay, yeah. I get it.

DOMINIQUE. "Hey, can you get condoms for this weekend?" Don't you just think it will make me look weird?

JOEY. I get how it looks to everyone, you know?

JULIE. Yeah, it actually does sound like you're *Fifty Shades of Grey*-ing it!

DOMINIQUE. Yes! I know! (*They laugh. And then look around hoping no one from school is there.*) It's just way too Linda Lovelace for me.

JULIE. Way too Joey Del Marco for you. (*They laugh.*)

JOEY. It's not fair you know, because they don't know what I was thinking when I bought them. They all think they're mind readers, these people, and they're not.

JULIE. Whatever. Does your mom have any?

DOMINIQUE. What?

JULIE. What if you just searched through the bathroom drawers or bedside tables or something?

DOMINIQUE. Yeah. I'm not doing that, okay? I'm not using condoms my mom uses with the guys she meets on fucking eHarmony, okay?

JULIE. Okay!

JOEY. Okay. But I want to say that I didn't plan it.

JULIE. Come on. (JULIE *heads toward the condom section of the pharmacy.*)

JOEY. I got the candy and then I was like, "I'm gonna get them. It'll be funny." So I just went over to the condom section. (DOMINIQUE *and* JULIE *stand in front of the condom aisle.*)

DOMINIQUE. Oh my god.

JULIE. What?

DOMINIQUE. The pharmacist is definitely judging me right now. Why do they put them right here so you have to feel like a total dirty girl?

JULIE. I guarantee you she doesn't think you're a dirty girl.

DOMINIQUE. Why the fuck are there so many options?

JULIE. The different types do different shit. Ribbed are supposed to be good I think. (*Dominique is horrified. Julie, amused, points to a pack.*) Get those.

DOMINIQUE. Which ones?

JOEY. I got the ones I got not because I'm kinky or something but because it was a joke.

JULIE. The red and blue pack.

DOMINIQUE. (*She leans in to look.*) No! I don't want any kinky fire and ice shit. I'm not looking for fireworks, okay? I just want the basics.

JOEY. God . . .

JULIE. Oh my god, look!

DOMINIQUE. Shhh!

JULIE. Right there. Those are them. Flavored condoms. Oh my god, that's unbelievable. I mean, I would have killed to see the look on the cashier's face when she brought those up to the register.

DOMINIQUE. It probably turned him on.

JOEY. I didn't do it to turn them on. It wasn't like that. I mean, when you really think about it, how can flavored condoms be anything *but* a joke?

DOMINIQUE. Poor Joey.

JULIE. Joey Blow Me.

JOEY. Joey Blow Me. Not that clever, actually. Sort of fifth grade but . . . you know . . .

DOMINIQUE. Dude, stop.

JULIE. I'm just kidding, come on.

JOEY. But . . . you know . . . it still makes me feel like shit. It still sucks when your dad sees that shit online. (*Beat.*) And he looks at you like you're not you anymore . . . (*Beat.*) Yeah, I'm okay. Whatever. So, pretty much everyone thinks I bought them because I was planning on giving them all blow jobs and I wanted the blow jobs to taste like, I don't know, a rainbow of fruit flavors, I guess.

DOMINIQUE. (*She walks away from the section and motions for* JULIE *to follow her.*) Come here . . . come over here! My stomach is like flipping its shit . . . literally. I can't. I can't just stand there for, like, ten minutes in front of there and debate and discuss. Let's just talk about it over here.

JULIE. I don't think the ribs will hurt. I think they're small. They're just supposed to add, like, friction or something so it feels better? Maybe that's actually good? Just get those!

DOMINIQUE. Fine, fine . . . okay.

JULIE. What size?

DOMINIQUE. I have no idea.

JULIE. Dude, are you telling me you haven't seen his dick because, honestly, he's gonna put that in you and—

DOMINIQUE. No, no, no, no. I have, I have . . . obviously. But I don't, um, I don't really have anything to compare it to. I mean, how many penises do you think I've seen? I'm not a fucking whore.

JOEY. I mean people actually think I'm a fucking whore because of these condoms. Like I was actually going to blow three guys! Who would ever really do that? And it seems like you're saying that their opinion is, like, a big deal . . .

JULIE. Show me how big it is? (DOMINIQUE *reluctantly shows the size with her hands.*)

DOMINIQUE. Is that small? (JULIE *thinks for a second.*) Is it?

JULIE. I have no fucking idea! Fuck this, Dom. Just go to the nurse.

JOEY. If people could just understand where I was coming from, they would get it, maybe. I mean, maybe we could even call in the school nurse.

DOMINIQUE. Not possible! Not happening—never. I can't stand her face.

JOEY. Because that's how all of this started—with the condoms! Okay, because, okay—we were in health and she was leading a class about reproduction and, like, you know, everyone turned it into a sex talk.

DOMINIQUE. I don't want a sex lecture, or whatever.

JOEY. And Miss Garrison has this whole mission in health class. She doesn't want us to be afraid to ask questions.

DOMINIQUE. She acts like she's all cool, but she's not. She'll treat me like I'm making a bad decision. And she's always like, "no judgment," but that's bullshit.

JOEY. She lets us pass up anonymous questions at the end of class and the guys constantly try to throw her by asking something over-the-top sexual. But she never freaks out.

DOMINIQUE. Okay, I'm starting to freak out! What do I do?

JULIE. I don't know but . . . you're running out of time, babe, because I gotta go soon. I told Mari and Katie I'd meet them at six.

DOMINIQUE. (Sighs.) Fine . . . okay. What are you guys doing?

JULIE. Watching *Frozen*.

DOMINIQUE. I can't believe you're watching that again without me.

JULIE. So blow off Dylan and have a girls' night with us. You love girls' night!

DOMINIQUE. I can't . . . but I'm jealous.

JULIE. 'Cause girls' night kills it. Zero stress. I'm gonna get my Kristen Bell on, bitch. I'm gonna be all, like, (*sings*) "Do you wanna build a snowman . . ."

DOMINIQUE. (*Loving it, but trying to keep her quiet.*) Okay, okay, okay! Lovely . . . Hey, please promise you're not gonna tell them we were doing this today.

JULIE. Are you kidding? Dude, I would never do that. Come on. Just go over there, grab the first pack you see, and go to the checkout. I swear to god, no one gives a shit. Just do it.

JOEY. But these guys—Luke and Tim included—are idiots. They are really twelve years old. And they pass up a note that says, "Could you please explain the benefits of flavored condoms? I recently bought some grape-flavored ones and I'd be grateful for your advice."

DOMINIQUE. I wish I was one of those girls, you know? Someone who can just be, like, "Yup, I'm here to buy a pack of condoms because I'm going to have sex with my boyfriend, who I really love . . . "

JOEY. You would have loved it. Because she just says, "Some people use flavored condoms because it may make oral sex more pleasurable for the giver. They still successfully protect against pregnancy and STDs. The only warning I would issue is that sometimes novelty condoms can cause vaginal irritation."

DOMINIQUE. "And there's nothing wrong with that. I'm not some dumb little teenage whore. And I'll take the ribbed *and* the plain because I don't know what I like yet. And you can just deal with it, okay? Great."

JOEY. Great, right? I mean . . . the guys, Tim, Luke, Farid, Derek—I can name them all if you want—they went nuts. They were dying laughing.

DOMINIQUE. Why can't I do that? Like, it's no big deal. You know what I mean? You know those girls?

JULIE. Yeah, but those girls get themselves into Joey Del Marco situations.

JOEY. Does it make sense now—the condom situation? Tim, Luke, and George know it was a joke. I mean, we were reenacting Miss Garrison's whole speech! And now they're saying . . . I mean if they're saying that—

DOMINIQUE. What are you saying?

JULIE. I'm saying, Joey's all like, "I own my sexuality. Yeah I hook up, and I'm a badass, and I'm part of the Slut Squad"—and look where it got her. It landed her in the backseat of a cab with a group of guys who think she wanted it because, to be honest, she pretty much acts like she does, does she not?

DOMINIQUE. I don't know. It's like, we don't even know her really.

JULIE. I'm not talking shit, I'm just saying . . .

JOEY. There are pictures of me tasting the condoms online. I know that. And I hate that, okay? I'm, like, seriously upset about that. My parents . . . I mean, I can't even believe I did that. So it's stupid, okay? I'm aware. But everyone's acting like it's beyond fucked up. But . . . I'm not the only person with pictures like that. Is that really worse than a friend of mine who has a picture of herself online smoking a blunt? Or, like, blowing a banana?

JULIE. So, what? You're not talking to me now?

DOMINIQUE. What? No . . . no. I'm just surprised . . . that's all.

JOEY. I'm not surprised they took the pictures. Not totally shocking. But . . . *they* did it too. Did you see the pictures of *them*? You have those, right? So, am I not allowed to make stupid jokes, too?

DOMINIQUE. I mean, isn't she allowed to act like she wants it as much as she wants without, you know . . .

JULIE. I mean, can you imagine how fucking bad that was? No wonder she puked all over herself at Connor's.

DOMINIQUE. Dude, yes.

JOEY. I hate myself for doing it. Why did I do it? I ask myself that all the time. I don't even sleep because of that, you know. And I think, man, if I hadn't bought those things would it have even happened?

DOMINIQUE. I think they did it.

JOEY. Was that the one big trigger factor?

JULIE. So do I. But she *did* put herself in a fucked situation.

JOEY. I mean, do you think it was?

DOMINIQUE. Yeah, but I've put myself in fucked-up situations before.

JULIE. Oh, fuck yeah. Me too.

JOEY. And it's like, does that really invite what happened? You know? Buying the condoms made me seem into it—along with everything else about me, I guess. I understand how it looks. It's just not fair. It's bullshit.

JULIE. It's actually such bullshit 'cause every guy I know acts like he's all into sex and I've never heard of a group of girls holding him down and jerking him off, or sticking their fingers up some orifice. Except for in porn.

DOMINIQUE. (*Motivated.*) Okay, I'm getting them. I'm totally doin' it! The cashier can get over it.

JULIE. Dude, I think you're the one who needs to get over it.

DOMINIQUE. Fuck you.

JULIE. Nice. Hey, I'm getting this . . . what do you think? (*She holds up lip gloss and shows her lips.*)

DOMINIQUE. Do it. (DOMINIQUE *and* JULIE *exit. Lights dim stage left.*)

JOEY. So . . . we were messing around with the condoms and drinking at the same time. Yes, that's when the pictures were taken. I didn't know they uploaded them, no. But it's not like I would have been able to control that anyway . . . And I just wasn't thinking about . . . the impact of them . . . in that moment. I was drunk . . . (*Beat.*) Then I started getting texts from all my friends on the dance team saying they were on their way to the party. So we sort of cleaned up—got rid of the bottles and Luke took the opened condoms to his room because he didn't want his mom to find them in the trash. George stuffed the rest of them in his coat pocket and we left . . . No, we didn't even think of taking the subway. We just started looking for a cab. It was freezing. And I had bare legs. There was no way I was walking to the subway. We finally found a cab at, like, 9:30-ish. I remember the time because I texted my friend Jane telling her I was in the cab. You have that from my phone records, right? (*Beat.*) Yes, I'm on the dance team. I'm a junior, so it's my third year on the team. I think I could probably be captain next year . . . Yes. Does that matter? . . . Okay . . . Yes, I understand . . . Yes . . . The Slut Squad.

SCENE 4: SLUTTIN' IT UP

SCENE: *Lights up stage left as the* SLUT SQUAD *enters the locker room, now projected on the screen, after a Saturday night basketball game. They're not really talking to one another much. They start to get their stuff together.* JOEY'S *statement intertwines with the* SLUT SQUAD'S *dialogue.*

NATALIE. (*To* DANIELLE.) What are you doing?

DANIELLE. Wha—

NATALIE. Were you about to fucking come in here? (DANIELLE *stops dead in her tracks.*) Are freshmen allowed in here right now?

DANIELLE. No.

GRACE. So, stay out there. Right there. See that line? Don't cross that line until we're done. You wait in the doorway until we're done. Or did you forget that, Danielle?

NATALIE. I'm exhausted. (*She sighs.*) I cannot wait to get home . . . I'm gonna watch TV and do nothing. Did I tell you my dad is, like, obsessed with—(CHRISTINA *is making a show of shoving her stuff in her bag. She's clearly pissed at the others.*) Is there a problem or something, Christina?

CHRISTINA. Nope.

NATALIE. Really? (CHRISTINA *ignores her.*)

JOEY. Really? You think this is going to be an issue too? . . . How? (*Beat.*) Wow.

GRACE. Silent treatment. That's pretty ridiculous.

JOEY. It's just so ridiculous to me, you know? I don't know . . . this is . . . I'm just feeling sort of . . . I feel like every little aspect of my life is being ripped into with all of this . . . I know. I'm sorry that I keep, like . . . It's just, in any other scenario, you know.

CHRISTINA. Okay. You wanna know what's pissing me off?

NATALIE. Sure.

CHRISTINA. That was our worst performance of the season, mainly because you were fucking off. Every fucking time you do your new sequence, you're off.

NATALIE. What?

CHRISTINA. And it looks like shit.

NATALIE. Are you kidding me?

CHRISTINA. And no matter how many times Coach told you you weren't hitting the kick, no matter how many times she, like, drilled that with you, you still couldn't get it. What's your problem? It looked really fucking bad.

GRACE. Chrissy, she just learned it on Tuesday!

CHRISTINA. I don't give a fuck. She shouldn't even be doing it.

NATALIE. You. Are. Such. A. Bitch.

JOEY. When I started at Elliot, the dance team was already called the Slut Squad. I actually don't even know how long ago that started. So it's not like it was all our idea. It's just sort of a nickname; like

SLUT: THE PLAY   123

in my cousin's school, there's a group of girls who call themselves the Dirty Dozen. It's just what the group of friends is known as. It's the same thing for us.

NATALIE. So I guess you think you should be doing it, right? You would have saved the day, right?

CHRISTINA. I think Joey should be doing it!

NATALIE. Well . . . in case you haven't heard . . . Joey was a little busy slutting herself out a couple of weeks ago so, unfortunately, she's no longer here with her perfect on-beat kicks.

GRACE. Jesus Nat—

NATALIE. So if you wanna be pissed at someone for tonight, Chrissy, be pissed at Joey.

JOEY. Are there requirements for being in the Slut Squad? . . . Well, yeah, you have to be on the dance team. That's pretty much it.

CHRISTINA. Well, that was pretty much the worst shit we've ever done.

GRACE. And it's not Natalie's fault, Christina. I mean, what the hell?

CHRISTINA. "What the hell?" Grace? We go out there, after all this shit with Joey, and the guys can't even keep the game *close* without Luke, and *she* dances like that—it's all fucking weak.

NATALIE. You're seriously overreacting.

CHRISTINA. Really? Well (*pointing toward* DANI-ELLE), that fucking freshman right there danced circles around you, so, hey if you're cool with that . . .

JOEY. It's sort of like a sorority . . . Is there hazing? No. Definitely not. I mean we're a little hard on the freshmen but it's just 'cause we want them to pay their dues, you know.

NATALIE. I'm telling you, Danielle, if you even smile a little . . .

JOEY. Stupid stuff like they have to wait until after we change to come in the locker room. And they can only speak when spoken to, which we honestly don't even really enforce because we like them. They're cute. And they have to go on Starbucks runs and dance in the back. It's not anything serious.

GRACE. Okay, so we fucked up a little. It was just the middle section. The opening was amazing.

CHRISTINA. Did you hear those kids from Leighton chanting in the left section?

NATALIE. Why are you doing this tonight?

GRACE. What were they saying?

CHRISTINA. I swear to god, I want to kill that dick Mark. You know he's Sam Beekman's cousin, right? I want to kill him and that whole crew of Leighton slut-bags he's always with at games.

NATALIE. Yeah, me too.

CHRISTINA. Well, why are you acting like you don't even care?

NATALIE. I *do* care but—

GRACE. Wait. What Mark guy?

NATALIE. He's that fat kid from Leighton. He's always in the stands with the red and gold Leighton sweatshirt and that fucking ski hat. I want to rip that fucking hat off his greasy fat head. He's an asshole because he's not on the team and it's the only way he can get girls.

GRACE. Okay. So what did he say?!

CHRISTINA. Unbelievable.

DANIELLE. "Leighton'll have you crying RAPE like a SLUT in the back of a cab—NO ESCAPE!" (*They all stare at her.*)

JOEY. It's not called the Slut Squad because we're actually, like, sluts . . . like in that way. No one is pressured to have sex . . . No. I mean, no . . . No one is, like, pressured into any type of sexual activity. I mean that would be so twisted . . . it's just not like that.

NATALIE. They were referencing Joey. Not us.

CHRISTINA. They're referencing the Slut Squad, are you kidding me?

JOEY. That's not even what "slut" really means to us.

GRACE. I can't believe Mr. Dowerly didn't say anything to them. They should have been kicked out for that.

CHRISTINA. They're saying we're a bunch of all-talk sluts who cry rape when things get tough.

NATALIE. Well, it's not true. When have I cried rape, Chris? Huh? (*Beat.*) When I hook up with someone, I take total responsibility for that, like anyone should . . . Unless it's like actually rape, okay? And don't get me wrong. I may not always be like, "Oh, awesome, I'm so totally proud of that choice!" But I don't pussy out and blame the guy.

Neither does Grace, or you—or like any girl on this team. Not even the freshman—right, Dani?

DANIELLE. Yeah. (GRACE *shoots* DANIELLE *a look*.)

NATALIE. What?

DANIELLE. Nothing.

JOEY. When I think of what our idea of "slut" is on the team, and I know it sounds stupid now but . . . it's positive. We think it's wrong that guys can hook up with whoever they want and that's totally cool, but girls can't. It's an unfair double standard. So we're like, "Hey, if we act confident about sex and . . ."

NATALIE. (*To* DANIELLE.) We own our shit.

JOEY. "And we aren't afraid to be sexual. If all that makes us sluts, then I guess we're sluts." So, Slut Squad just means we're confident and, you know, sexy.

CHRISTINA. It's just that no one sees us that way anymore, Nat. Not since this. And it's humiliating. (*Beat*.)

GRACE. Have you talked to her?

CHRISTINA. Who, Joey?

GRACE. Yeah.

CHRISTINA. No. Have you?

GRACE. No.

NATALIE. I definitely haven't.

GRACE. She called me after she left Connor's, like five times.

NATALIE. Trying to get her story straight, I'm sure.

JOEY. It's only been after this that I've been called a slut in the way that means I'm really a dirty whore.

CHRISTINA. Yeah, well . . . whatever.

JOEY. I haven't talked to the girls on the team at all.

CHRISTINA. I don't want junior year to be like this now. With the fucking SATs coming up! Seriously. Fuck her, man.

JOEY. They just don't want to be a part of all of this, I'm sure.

NATALIE. And I mean, we're totally screwed for the rest of the season, right?

CHRISTINA. I just don't get why she's doing all this.

JOEY. No, none of them talked to me at the party. I mean, there's a good chance they just didn't even know what was going on. There were, like, forty people there, or something. But, no, we haven't talked since earlier that night.

GRACE. I feel bad.

JOEY. I sort of feel bad about that. Obviously. They're my friends so . . . I'm pretty sure that means they don't believe me . . . which I mean . . .

CHRISTINA. Honestly, that's, like, the only thing I have to say to her, Grace: Why. Are. You. Doing. This?

NATALIE. For the attention.

GRACE. She doesn't need to do that for attention.

NATALIE. Why are you defending her, Grace?

GRACE. I'm not!

CHRISTINA. Do you really think they raped her, Grace? Rape?

GRACE. I don't know.

NATALIE. Come on.

GRACE. Those guys can be like . . . (*Trying to figure out how to say it.*) . . . George . . . I mean . . . I . . .

NATALIE. Your ex-boyfriend is a rapist. That's what you're saying?

GRACE. No, Nat . . .

CHRISTINA. I've known Joey since kindergarten. She loses control sometimes. She's done weird shit before. That night I think she got back to her house with Jane, and her parents were there, and she just started lying, you know?

NATALIE. Yeah.

JOEY. So you think the fact that my dance team is called the Slut Squad is going to make people think that I must be an actual slut—

CHRISTINA. And she's really screwed over the whole school.

JOEY. They'll say I'm "admittedly promiscuous"? I hate the word promiscuous. (*Beat.*) So that implies what? That I couldn't have been . . . you know . . . raped, then? That cancels out the possibility of rape to people? (*Beat.*) That's . . . crazy.

NATALIE. So what should we do?

JOEY. So what should I do?

CHRISTINA. Get our shit together 'cause another night like this can't happen. And don't talk about

Joey. No more online shit either. I don't wanna be associated with her.

NATALIE. Okay.

CHRISTINA. And, Nat, you seriously gotta work on that sequence or give it away. 'Cause it's just pulling us down even more. For real.

NATALIE. Fine. (*Her phone rings.*) Hold on. (NATALIE *answers her phone.*) Hi Mom . . . Yeah, it was okay . . . No, it's just a bad night. We lost. No, yeah, I'm good . . . Yeah, tell Dad to wait for me. Uh—Pepperoni? Okay, I'm coming home now. Love you. (*She hangs up.*) You'll work on it with me Monday? (CHRISTINA *nods. They hug goodbye. Say "Love ya's." NATALIE exits.*)

CHRISTINA. Bye Gracie. (*To* DANIELLE.) You did a good job, tonight, you know? (DANIELLE *nods.* CHRISTINA *exits.*)

JOEY. You know, I feel like everything I've ever done is so stupid.

GRACE. (*To* DANIELLE.) You thinking about Silas?

DANIELLE. No.

GRACE. You never told them about that, I guess, right?

DANIELLE. No.

GRACE. Hey, he's an idiot.

DANIELLE. Yeah.

GRACE. You know, George once followed me into the bathroom and locked the door and wouldn't let me out until I gave him a hand job. True story. I didn't tell anyone. We ended up going out for, like, five months . . .

JOEY. All I want to do is, like . . . cry . . . No. Actually even better. Go back in time. I wish I could go back in time. Someone needs to invent a time machine now.

GRACE. (*Starts to leave.*) You can go in now. Hey, I mean, you know Christina and Natalie aren't really like that, obviously. They're just worried about the team, you know? (DANIELLE *nods and* GRACE *heads for the door.*)

DANIELLE. (*She stops* GRACE, *obviously uncomfortable.*) Wait. Grace—I wanted to tell you that . . . um . . . I'm quitting the team. I just . . . I don't know . . . my schedule is just too nuts and I really can't keep up anymore, so I'm going to tell Coach that I—

GRACE. You can't. Sorry. There's too much going on right now and we really need you. Sorry. You can't quit, okay? (DANIELLE *just stares at* GRACE *as she leaves.*) Hey, good job, tonight! See you Monday. (DANIELLE *just stands there.*)

JOEY. This is just getting worse. (DANIELLE *exits. Lights dim stage left.*) So, that's the deal with the Slut Squad . . . Oh, sure. Of course. No problem. I'm totally fine, yeah . . . No, I'm good. Okay . . . (JOEY *watches the Assistant District Attorney leave the room. She is alone for a moment . . . she breathes, puts her head on the table. She hears the door open . . . her visitor catches her by surprise.*) Hey Dad . . . I'm good . . . Yeah, she just stepped out for a second to use the bathroom . . . Yeah, I'm just tired. What's Mom doing? . . . Okay, good . . . It's going okay, I think, but I don't really know . . . It's just— everyone pretty much hates me, Dad, and I don't know . . . I'm really sorry about all of this, Dad . . . I know . . . (*She smiles a little—tries to prove she's "okay."*) I know . . . Yeah, I'm fine . . . You should go . . . 'Cause I can hear her coming back . . . Okay—okay . . . just go, okay? . . . I know . . . I love you too . . . Yeah, I'm gonna be fine . . . Love you. (JOEY *watches her dad leave. The Assistant District Attorney is back.*) Hi. Yeah, my dad just popped his head in to say "hi." They're just worried, you know . . . but I'm okay. So, okay . . . So, I found a cab after about five minutes . . . On 8th Avenue. Right on the corner of 8th and Horatio, and we all got in the backseat. (JOEY *drinks her water and composes herself.*) I remember the driver was black—but, um, African. Not African American, but actually he was from Africa, I think. I'm sorry. I sound like such a jerk, right? I'm sorry. He had an African name, I know that. Like . . . Batuba, or something, but it wasn't Batuba. I don't really remember specifically what he looked like. He was very dark skinned and had a shaved head and no facial hair. Maybe he was, like, fortyish. Do you think there's any way to track him down? I mean, if I saw him I might recognize him. Don't they have to submit a log or something? Is it possible to trace the starting and ending points of our trip or whatever, or. . . Okay, yeah . . . He had an accent, I know that, and he was playing music pretty loud.

SCENE 5: BROS BEFORE HOS

SCENE: *Lights come up stage left on* ANNA *in her bedroom. Loud music is playing. She is wearing pajamas and reading something on her computer. Her brother Tim knocks on her door. Anna doesn't hear him at first.* JOEY *continues with her statement; the stories intertwine.*

JOEY. And I remember Tim asked him to turn it down a little.

ANNA. (*She looks up and sees Tim.*) What?

JOEY. And the guy completely ignored him.

ANNA. (*Turns down the music.*) What's up? . . . Okay, well it's down now so . . .

JOEY. Yes, so it was Tim, Luke, me, then George. And, sort of, in order for us all to fit comfortably . . .

ANNA. What?

JOEY. I just sort of slung my leg over George's.

ANNA. Nothing.

JOEY. It was nothing. I mean my dress was still covering me, you know?

ANNA. Just, you know looking at Facebook and stuff. (*Beat.*) Okay. Hey—can you shut the door? (*She heads back to her computer and sees that he hasn't left.*) What? . . .

JOEY. What were we doing?

ANNA. Why? What's she doing? . . .

JOEY. Just hanging out, you know, and—

ANNA. Is she yelling at Dad or just crying again?

JOEY. We were sort of talking, but the music was pretty loud.

ANNA. Well . . . what do you want her to do? . . . This is all like . . . bad, Tim, and . . .

JOEY. It wasn't bad right away.

ANNA. She loves you . . . so . . . it's just . . . bad.

JOEY. I don't even know how it all happened.

ANNA. How am I looking at you? . . . No, I'm not . . . I haven't at all! . . . I have not. The past three weeks, all I do is go to school, and pick up Thea, come home and you guys are always huddled in the kitchen or somewhere, and I'm not a part of any of this. Then come in and shut the door then—but I haven't been looking at you like anything! . . . No . . . I'm just . . . Tim, you know . . . you're my brother (*She has a hard time saying this.*) . . . and I'm really worried about you . . . (*She tries to compose herself.*)

JOEY. Yeah, I'm okay. It's just—I hate this . . . aspect of it the most. I think about it all the time, but saying it out loud . . .

ANNA. I mean . . . did you do it? . . . Yes, I know what you said! I *do* believe you. I mean, you're like my best—(*Beat.*) But, if you didn't do anything, then why were you fucking arrested, and you're on academic probation, and—

JOEY. I sort of don't understand how I should say all of this? I should say all the details right?

ANNA. So tell me, then . . . just tell me what happened, because . . . Mom and Dad know the details, and the lawyers, but I don't know anything, and I'm at school all day hearing all this stuff, and we haven't talked about it, and. . . Okay . . . Okay, I know. . . . I'm sorry. . . . So—tell me.

JOEY. We were kind of dancing in the back, and George was sort of keeping the beat on my leg, you know, sort of like, I know this sounds weird, but playing drums on my leg.

ANNA. Yes, I know how Joey gets when she's drunk.

JOEY. And then George and I started to, like . . . make out for a second, but it was only for a second, and then he started to put his hand up my leg.

ANNA. But, I also know how *you guys* get when you're drunk.

JOEY. I just sort of slapped it away, like, in a friendly way, but then he did it again but . . . this time his hand actually went up my dress and sort of grazed my crotch. (*Beat.*) I guess I started to get nervous at that point. My heart started really beating, and I remember tightening up and kind of clamping down on his hand with my hand. (*Beat.*) I looked at him and he was looking sort of past me at Luke with this face on. I mean, I don't know how to describe the face, but, sort of like "Hey, man, look what *I'm* doing." So I said, "George, come on, stop. Just wait until we get to Connor's." . . . I'm not sure I said "stop," exactly, but I mean it was clear that I wanted him to stop because I was trying to pull my leg down off his, you know? And I was trying to push his hand off me, but he was grabbing my skin, sort of clawing it a little. (*Beat.*) I don't know. I don't know if I actually would have done anything with him at Connor's. I was just saying that so he would stop doing the stuff right there in the cab. I was trying to offer something up, you know? It seemed like a good idea at the time . . . (*She takes a sip of water.*)

ANNA. Nothing . . . Sorry, nothing . . . I'm just picturing her you know . . . Sorry, so then what?

JOEY. So then, next thing I know, Luke is grabbing my other leg . . . Pulling my leg to the side, so my, um, legs would be more open and George—then George kind of moved his body so *his* leg was on top of my leg, sort of pinning me down. It was pretty much impossible for me to move because their bodies were pressing my arms against the back of the seat—like this. So my arms are like this, and George starts pulling at my dress, pulling it up farther. (*She drinks water.*) Like, how much detail do you need?

ANNA. I hate thinking of her struggling. George and Luke are so much bigger than her. I would have been beside myself—hysterical, being, like, pinned down by the two of them. I would have been screaming like a psycho. I don't get them.

JOEY. Then George all of a sudden really aggressively pulls my underwear to the side and jammed two of his fingers inside me. (*Beat.*)

ANNA. That's disgusting. (*Beat.*) So, what did you do? . . . What did you do when they started doing that?

JOEY. I was crying at this point, but I didn't scream. I just couldn't. I couldn't make a scream come out. It felt like I was choking.

ANNA. And the driver didn't notice anything?

JOEY. The music was pretty loud, like I said, so the driver, I guess, just couldn't hear anything. I remember just staring so hard into the rearview mirror, wondering if he would catch my eye. I was horrified at the thought. I was so embarrassed. I mean, I was disgusting. My vagina was pretty exposed, and I kept thinking if this guy turns around to check on us and sees me like this, we're going to get in an accident.

ANNA. Why didn't you stop the cab?

JOEY. George had his fingers in me . . . Two . . . Yes, I'm sure . . . Because I saw them! (*Beat.*) Okay, so, and he was sort of—uh, um—moving them in and out as hard as he could and as fast as he could. Kind of in a stabbing motion. And he was really putting his whole body into it, and I was . . . I was clenching pretty hard, does that make sense? I was squeezing everything, trying to sort of close myself up . . . and I think that made it hurt even more. And I'm crying. And the whole time Luke is making fun of George because I'm . . . you know . . . you know . . . because I'm not coming. Because I'm not having an orgasm. He was laughing and saying, like, "Dude, do you even know what the fuck you're doing? You're giving the poor girl fucking pussy burn. You make girls cry you're so bad at that shit." That type of stuff, and George was like, "Fuck you—it's not me—" And then he said . . . he said, "Her pussy's as dry as a fucking desert." (*Beat.*) He finally pulled his fingers out. Luke was laughing and he was bragging how he was going to show George how it was done. Then he put two of his fingers in his mouth. And I just really started to go crazy because I knew what was coming and . . . that's when George said, "I feel like we're fucking wrestling an alligator or some shit."

ANNA. Did he seriously say that?

JOEY. (*Visibly shaken.*) I need a second, okay? (*She tries to breathe.*) So George says the alligator thing and then Luke laughs—and then he stuck his wet fingers in my vagina. (*She has a hard time with this next sentence.*) He told me he wet his fingers because I was so dry. (*Beat.*) Then he did the same thing as George except he was trying to show off. I was hysterically crying, and he kept saying things like, "Come on JoJo—you know you wanna come— you know you're wet now." And then he seemed to get tired or, I don't know, annoyed with me, and he said, "Wow—guess you're all talk, huh, Joey?" And he and George laughed. Luke pulled his fingers out of me and wiped them on George's shirt. And then they let go of me. (*Beat.*)

ANNA. I hate them.

JOEY. I hate them whenever I think about it.

ANNA. That is the most fucked up thing I've ever heard. I don't understand. She said, "No," right?

JOEY. Yes, during the whole thing I kept saying, "Come on you guys. Don't. No. No, I don't want to do this."

ANNA. So what were *you* doing?

JOEY. Tim was just looking out the window.

ANNA. Why didn't you do anything? . . . You sat there, Tim. You didn't stop the cab. You didn't text anyone. You didn't even say anything to them! . . . Um, like, "What the hell are you guys doing? Stop." . . . But you were a part of it! You were right there while two of your best friends were doing crazy shit to a girl you've known your whole life, and she clearly wasn't into it.

JOEY. I really don't want him to get in trouble for this. He's a good guy and he works really hard and stuff. And he's one of my really good friends. I think he just probably didn't know what to do and that's not his fault. He's the twin brother of one of my best friends, you know? Anna. I haven't talked to her since this.

ANNA. But, I mean, you looked at your phone and stared out the fucking window. Why? . . . Maybe you were drunker than you thought?

JOEY. I don't feel very well.

ANNA. Because you *know* her! She's one of my best friends. She's gone camping with us, Tim.

JOEY. I'm sorry. How much longer do you think we'll be?

ANNA. You're right, I really don't get it. . . . Were you afraid they were going to hurt you or something? I mean, I know what they're like when they're drunk. Like that time in Brooklyn when Luke took that rock from in front of the church on Clinton Street and then smashed the window of that car. That was fucking crazy. He was out of control. Did you think they would—

JOEY. No . . . I'm okay—I'm fine to keep going . . .

ANNA. Okay! So then tell me. Because I know you better than anyone and you're not like this. (*Quieting her voice so the rest of the family doesn't hear.*) And I keep thinking about Thea, Tim, and how we'd literally kill anyone who ever did anything close to that to her. I mean picture her. Not knowing what to do and feeling scared and trapped. And that's how Joey felt and . . . you just didn't help her. And you're an awesome guy. And you may have just fucked your whole life. And that's why this whole thing is a fucking nightmare, or something, because you are NOT that guy.

JOEY. The last thing I remember seeing before it started was Columbus Circle mall.

ANNA. I know it happened fast.

JOEY. When they were done we were at 78th and Lex. I saw the street sign. No—

ANNA. No, I won't—tell me.

JOEY. I didn't get out. I should have, I guess. But I didn't know what to do. My underwear was ripped and I was sore. I just stared at the taxi TV. (*Beat.*) They tried to talk to me, you know? They teased me for ignoring them. Luke put his arm around me and said, "Give me a hug. You're, like, the most down girl ever." . . . No, Tim didn't join the conversation. He was still just looking out the window.

ANNA. (*She stares at him. The answer surprises her.*) You didn't want to be a pussy. (*Beat.*)

JOEY. The cab pulled up to Connor's building. I gave ten bucks.

ANNA. That's totally fucked. And I believe you, Tim. And I understand and I love you a lot, okay? (*Beat.*) But you gotta know that's totally fucked. "Guys don't do that to other guys." (*Beat.*)

JOEY. I locked myself in the bathroom when I got there. And I threw up everywhere.

ANNA. (*Trying to understand her brother.*) Because, so what if they called you a pussy? What would have happened? Would you have lost them as friends, do you think? Would you have died? (*Beat.*) So then don't be a pussy, Tim.

JOEY. Jane helped me. I told her what happened and she gave me her underwear. We called my mom and then we got in a cab. We got to my house at 10:45-ish.

ANNA. Why would the lawyers say that?

JOEY. I told my parents. My mom put my underwear in a ziplock baggie. I think she thought there was "evidence" on them but . . . you know. They were really good about it. My dad cried, which really made me cry.

ANNA. But that stuff doesn't matter 'cause you know they did it.

JOEY. I know they're disappointed, you know?

ANNA. Yes, more than anything, obviously, I want what's gonna be best for *you*. I just don't understand how that's right, though. (ANNA *hears her mom call to her; she takes a breath.*)

ANNA. Yeah, Mom? . . . He's right here . . . Okay . . . We're coming. (*She looks at him. They share an "our mom is annoying and losing it" look.*) I hate our family like this . . . (*Beat.*) Go . . . Yeah, I'm okay. I'm just realizing I'm probably never going to talk to Joey again, right? (ANNA *exits. Lights dim stage left.*)

JOEY. Ten to fifteen minutes. Everything happened in only, like, ten to fifteen minutes. That's it. That's all it took for my life to . . . just . . . implode. (*Beat.*) And now I'm Slutty Girl who shouldn't have gotten drunk, and shouldn't have been there, and shouldn't have done all the things that everyone says I shouldn't have done. But how is it all about everything *I* shouldn't have done? So now I'm that girl.

SCENE 6: RAPE GIRLS

SCENE: *Lights come up stage left on Starbucks.* SYLVIE *enters. She has a Starbucks cup and pastry bag. She settles herself in at a table, takes off her coat, and looks around. She's meeting someone.* JOEY *continues with her statement; the stories intertwine.*

JOEY. And I don't want to be.

SYLVIE. Thanks for meeting me here. I hope this isn't too random or, like, weird . . . Good . . . um, do you wanna get something? I got hot chocolate while I was waiting. Get in line if you want. Oh, okay . . . You sure?

JOEY. Sure . . . I mean, I *thought* I knew the point of doing all this, sure. But the thing is actually *doing* all this . . . is what makes me like that girl. The minute I went with my parents and Jane to the precinct that night; and the minute I filed the report; the minute they got arrested—I became her.

SYLVIE. I love your scarf. It looks really good on . . . did you make it? It looks homemade . . . Oh . . . Right . . . Yeah I love that place . . . You're welcome. So, when was the last time you saw Caroline? I honestly haven't seen her since that party she had. Which is crazy 'cause that was like freshman year, right? . . . Yeah . . . I mean we Facebook each other but . . . Yeah, it's weird because I met so many people at that party . . . I know! It was, like, the craziest party ever. And it's just funny because I'm better friends with some of the most random people I met there than I am with Caroline now . . . Yeah, we did, but then she left. She goes to, yeah, Bronx Science, yeah. I guess she likes it. I don't know.

JOEY. I know . . . I know, I understand . . . I know you are . . . And I really appreciate everything you guys are doing so much . . .

SYLVIE. So . . .

JOEY. So, I'm sorry if it ends up that I was just wasting all your time . . .

SYLVIE. How is everything going?

JOEY. Because . . . how do you think this is all going?

SYLVIE. I'm sorry. Am I an asshole for asking that? I just . . . I don't know what I should or shouldn't say and . . . (*She laughs awkwardly.*) Right, sure. Sorry, I'm just—

JOEY. No, I'm just asking. Because, I mean, do you really think anything will come of this? . . . Well, what does a really good chance mean? . . . But what do we have? . . . besides my ripped underwear, which you said doesn't exactly prove assault. It's basically what they say versus what I say, right? (*Beat.*)

SYLVIE. I saw what people were saying about you online and stuff and I . . .

JOEY. I lose then. I can see it happening.

SYLVIE. I just couldn't . . . it was really fucked up. People are, like, really twisted, huh?

JOEY. I lose!

SYLVIE. It's like you never think people will actually say such stupid shit, right?

JOEY. BECAUSE I'M A SLUT!

SYLVIE. I mean, you hear about it in the news.

JOEY. Haven't you heard? I mean, you didn't know that?

SYLVIE. But when you really see it and people you sorta know are writing it . . .

JOEY. I'm a whore.

SYLVIE. It's surreal. I'm sorry you've had to go through that. I'm just—really sorry. Seriously.

JOEY. But seriously, think of everything we just talked about! (*Beat.*) Who would you believe? Really. Be honest. I wouldn't even believe me, probably? So I'm a slut *and* a liar to everyone, you know? And it's like it doesn't matter what really happened, because no one will ever really know.

SYLVIE. It fucking sucks.

JOEY. And I'm just tired. And I don't want to do this! I'm tired of explaining everything. I know I probably should have to. I guess that's only fair. But I'm tired of it and I'm just . . . totally humiliated. And I . . . don't like my life like this! . . . I don't want it like this. I don't want my parents missing work to sit in a waiting room or to stay home with me because they're afraid I'm fucking suicidal or something. (*Beat.*) No . . . I'm not. I shouldn't have even said that. I'm sorry. I'm not at all. I'm . . . I'm . . . I'm just aware that I'm making their life awful and . . . everything they, you know, like, wanted for me . . .

SYLVIE. Have you been getting ready for the SATs? . . . I have this tutor. She's pretty good. I got the book, whatever. I just suck at standardized tests, you know? So bad news for me, huh? Bye bye Harvard, I guess, right? (*Awkwardly laughs.*) Exactly. I know. Do you have a list yet? . . . A college list? . . . My parents made me make one . . . Wesleyan? Really? . . . That's a really good school. That's awesome . . . Yeah . . . Well, if you apply early and get in, you don't need to worry about a list, right?

JOEY. I ruined all that by putting myself in the situation I did. (*Beat.*) And then coming forward . . . just made it all worse, actually.

SYLVIE. Actually . . . my brother goes to my dream college. I love the campus. I don't know, after being in the city my whole life, there's just something about a campus with Gothic buildings and trees and hills and nature and quiet—sounds so good to me. Sort of old school, you know? I just fell in love with it. Honestly, I don't even know if I'll be able to get in, that's the thing.

JOEY. I just don't know about this anymore! I mean, what do—what do you think will happen? . . . Seriously.

SYLVIE. Seriously, are you sure you don't want anything? Want a piece of my cookie?

JOEY. But, do you think Tim would do that? . . . Then why hasn't he done that yet? What's their thinking?

SYLVIE. You're probably thinking, "Why did this, like, random girl wanna hang out out of nowhere?"

JOEY. (*Shocked.*) Is it really possible that the charges will be dropped?

SYLVIE. Can I ask you a question?

JOEY. I keep asking myself . . .

SYLVIE. What made you say something? (*Beat.*) I mean, how did you, like, knowing that you were going to get so much shit coming at you.

JOEY. Over and over again—

SYLVIE. How did you do it?

JOEY. "Why did I do this?" If I hadn't reported it . . . it would be old news . . . I swear to god . . . it would have already been old news by now. It would have been this crazy, shitty thing that happened. No, no, actually, you know what? No one probably would have known but the guys and me because the only reason they started saying all that shit was because I *reacted* . . . I got all upset, and I left the party, and I wouldn't talk to them. So they went into major defense mode.

SYLVIE. Because I think it's really . . . I don't know . . . I think it's really brave. I don't know how you did it. I mean, you don't have to tell me . . . we don't even really know each other . . . I just—

JOEY. I just totally fucked myself.

SYLVIE. I don't know.

JOEY. No, I don't want them to come in right now. It's going to get them all upset and I just don't want to do that to them . . . (*Beat.*) I'm sorry, I'm really sorry. Obviously, I'm having some kind of panic thing. I'm really sorry. (*She tries to breathe.*) So, okay, if the charges don't get dropped, what will the story be?

SYLVIE. So, I went to visit my brother at school last year . . . He's a junior now. We're four years apart. I actually stayed there on campus with him and everything. Went to a really cool class on mid-twentieth century French film—totally what I'm into, and I was just really excited to be there. I slept right on the floor next to his bed. And we went to the local pizza place—just so good . . .

JOEY. Is that good? So, what would that scenario look like? . . . Okay, but if they cop a plea will the assault still be on their record? . . . What does it depend on? . . . So . . . What then, they'll . . . at the very, very least . . . (*Beat.*) Interesting. It will *always* be on *my* record . . . No, I mean . . . not technically but . . . in the minds of everyone that knows about this . . . I'll always be the girl from high school who claimed she was raped.

SYLVIE. The second night I was there, I was raped. (*Beat.*) Sorry to just throw that out there like that, but . . . I wanted you to know why I wanted to . . . to talk to you. I don't even use that word that much. 'Cause it's weird and even though that's what it was—and it was—I don't know . . . I just don't wanna be a rape girl, you know?

JOEY. I'm sorry.

SYLVIE. I mean, of course you know—duh. So I rarely use the word . . . I don't ever talk about it either . . . you know, to regular people.

JOEY. And they'll be regular people, back to partying every weekend . . . they'll be these poor wronged guys, back on the basketball team, back on the road to the Harvard dorms, right?

SYLVIE. My brother took me to a party at the dorm next to his. I honestly don't think I've ever been as excited and nervous and totally, like, pathetically insecure as I was that night. College parties are fucking ridiculous, okay. And my brother was like, "Please be fucking careful. I don't want to get in trouble because you're underage, and at this party, and drinking, and whatever. Just don't leave without me and don't leave the dorm. I don't want campus security seeing you. I'll be totally fucked if they catch you stumbling across campus, okay?" And that scared the shit out of me, but I was, like, "Yeah of course." (SYLVIE *sips and eats—as does* JOEY.)

JOEY. Next year I'm going to officially transfer to that school up near my grandparents upstate. It's a good school. But I'll be a senior, so I won't really have a chance to settle down there and fit in or whatever.

SYLVIE. I don't think I've ever tried so hard to fit in in my life. And the whole time I was like, "Damn it. I'm not wearing the right thing; I'm not saying the right shit; I look like I'm frigging thirteen. There's no way any of these guys will ever go for me. I'm such a loser." You know? It was just crazy. I remember this girl Jessica that was there, and I wanted to be her so bad. She was like the epitome of New England college girl hot you know? I could just tell she was, like, a Russian Lit major, or whatever, and she looked perfect smoking a joint and the guys were literally all over her. Anyway . . .

JOEY. So, in a way, we may all get the same punishment, the guys and me, for being bad . . .

SYLVIE. So I was bad. I smoked. I'd never smoked weed before and it just really fucked me up. I think maybe it was laced with something, because I was out of it. But I don't know, because I had never done it so I don't have anything to compare it to. But I was like funny-mirror-in-a-fun-house out of it, you know?

JOEY. I know . . .

SYLVIE. I knew I had to stay in the building, so I made my way down the hall. I wanted to get it together, you know? I found this room with a poster of Dwight from *The Office* on the door. I went in. No one was in it and it had a bathroom. I tried to make myself throw up, but it didn't work. I don't know if that would have made a difference.

JOEY. So, you know, is any of this really making a difference?

SYLVIE. Because I think the weed fucked me up. I had only had one drink.

JOEY. I mean, I went to my friend's house and had two drinks and—

SYLVIE. So then I splashed water on my face and just tried to get it together.

JOEY. Everything fell apart! And I'm, like, I feel like I'm at the bottom of this fucking pit—

SYLVIE. When I came out of the bathroom—

JOEY. And I can't get out of it at all.

SYLVIE. This kid was in the room. We started talking about, like, nothing, and then out of nowhere he just grabbed me and literally threw me on the bed. (*Beat.*) He didn't hit me or anything. Nothing like that. (*Beat.*) I know I said, "Stop." I didn't say "No." He leaned his whole upper body on my head and covered my mouth with his forearm. He smelled like beer. I mean, he didn't even look at me. (*Beat. SYLVIE sips to hide tears.*) And he . . . you know . . . (*Beat.*) I had never had sex before. And it was worse than I ever thought it would be, and I was sort of always scared of sex.

JOEY. I remember what I told you, yes!

SYLVIE. When he left the room, I got up and ran to the bathroom. I washed the shit out of my body and my mouth and everything.

JOEY. I told you I was angry.

SYLVIE. And it's weird because not even for a second did I think: DNA—don't wash yourself! I mean, I'd seen *SVU* like a thousand times, but I didn't even think about evidence, you know? I just wanted it off me, you know. (*She looks around to make sure no one is really listening.*) I remember feeling so glad that he didn't, you know, come in me, but I was freaked for weeks about STDs and getting pregnant. I kept examining myself for herpes or genital warts. I stayed up every night WebMD'ing myself to death.

JOEY. I was angry because . . . they . . . took something from me—

SYLVIE. So, anyway, I put my clothes on and walked out of the room and the party was fully going on.

JOEY. And they humiliated me and . . . made me feel like . . . a piece of shit! Like I was an idiot piece of trash.

SYLVIE. I mean, I knew I wasn't going to tell immediately. I played the whole thing out in my head.

JOEY. I told you that they were my friends . . . And that I felt they had betrayed me, and just completely violated me.

SYLVIE. Everyone would know—my brother, that Jessica girl—the school would know. They would never admit a girl who was, you know . . . you know, on their campus—an underaged girl who shouldn't have even been there. I was worried my brother would get in trouble and kicked out. And everyone at home would know. Other colleges. It would be on my record, or whatever. There was no way I could do it.

JOEY. And I'm pissed—

SYLVIE. That Jessica girl came up to me and told me my brother had gone to get more beer. She was just really sweet to me.

JOEY. Because they seemed to think they could do that to me. Like it was no big deal to them. (*Beat.*)

SYLVIE. The guy's name is Jeff. He graduated at the end of last year.

JOEY. And that's . . .

SYLVIE. I didn't tell my parents.

JOEY. Wrong. And I know it's wrong with, like, every little part of me.

SYLVIE. My brother and I don't talk as much now. I feel like he knows something. I did tell one of my friends and she didn't know what to say.

JOEY. I told you that I knew I had made some bad decisions and that I had put myself in not the best situation. But that, "so what?" I told you I had said, "No," and that I had begged them to stop. And they didn't and . . . no matter what I did. They were wrong. And you told me this would be hard and—and I said I didn't care—because—

SYLVIE. I think what you did was really . . . amazing.

JOEY. I am so fucking angry!

SYLVIE. I feel angry at myself. I think I regret not saying anything. (*Beat.*) Because . . .

JOEY & SYLVIE. It's so fucking infuriating . . .

SYLVIE. To know he's out there just happy and living his life and stuff. And maybe even doing it to someone else . . . and that's—

JOEY. I know. (*Beat. A moment of relief for* SYLVIE *and* JOEY.)

SYLVIE. I hate him, you know?

JOEY. Yes, I know.

SYLVIE. I mean, I think what you did . . .

JOEY. Yes, I do . . . No, I do . . . I do—believe in what I'm doing—yes.

SYLVIE. (*She looks at* JOEY.) Thank you for doing it, is what I want to say.

JOEY. I just wish it were different—you know . . . I don't know—I just wish that . . .

SYLVIE. I believe you. I wanted to tell you that. (JOEY *looks at* SYLVIE.)

(*Blackout.*)

THE END

Property List

Cell phones for all 11 characters

5 gym bags (JOEY, NATALIE, GRACE, CHRISTINA, DANIELLE)

Red Bull can (JOEY)

Makeup pouch (JOEY)

3 laptops (used by characters throughout)

Vodka bottle (JOEY)

Legal pad and pen (JOEY)

Bottle of water (JOEY)

Bagel or donut on a small paper plate (JOEY)

Twizzlers (LEILA/DANIELLE)

Box of condoms (DOMINIQUE)

Lip gloss (JULIE)

Starbucks coffee cup and cookie bag (SYLVIE)

Production Notes

The staging of *SLUT* should be clean, simple, honest, and fast-paced. The focus is kept on the actors, the text, and the power of the story. Set elements are minimalist: a desk, a chair, and a bench. (Rehearsal blocks are effective as a substitute.) There should be no attempt to design sets for each location.

After the prologue, Joey's storyline and those of girls in her community interweave, informing each other, playing side by side for the remainder of the play. Staging should support the intense purging of Joey's testimony, while clearly distinguishing the separate settings and character journeys for the audience. Thus, sound, light, and projections are major elements, constantly redefining the space and propelling the story forward.

Projections are a challenging undertaking but an essential component of the play. As we were told by our brilliant projection designer Grant McDonald, the most important questions to ask as you begin projection design for *SLUT* are: Why does this screen exist? What is the screen? Who does it belong to? How does it fit into the set? Remember that social media and smartphones often play crucial roles in the lives of young people and the mass sharing of information. To this point, we took time to create a "homemade" video of Joey and the boys (we found volunteer actors) pregaming: "drinking," dancing, and having fun. The footage functioned as an iPhone movie uploaded to a social media platform, and the video is played on the screen during the pregaming scene to provide context for the audience. Additionally, in all of our productions, we incorporated *live* video feed of Joey being interviewed, which was projected behind her onto the screen throughout the show. This effect helped add to the atmosphere of being "watched," under the community microscope, examined and distorted—as many young women experience when they come forward. To learn more about licensing the easily customizable projections used in the original National Tour of *SLUT*, please visit GrantMcDonald.com and click on "licensing."

Throughout the play, Joey and the others often speak to characters on the fourth wall. There should be no live actors filling those roles. The Assistant District Attorney, Jane's mom, Joey's dad, George, Luke, and Tim are not meant to have faces in any production of *SLUT*. (One exception: George, Luke, and Tim appear briefly in the pregaming video, if you decide to create one.)

Entrances and exits should be fast and seamless. Out of necessity, we experimented with having the actors enter and exit from different places throughout the audience—signifying that all the girls in the world of the play are constantly watching Joey from the moment she comes forward. It worked well, so we kept it. Feel free to do the same.

As you have read, there are a few cultural references in the play: *Friday Night Lights*, *Frozen*, Ask. FM, *Game of Thrones*, etc. Throughout our productions of *SLUT* we've had to update these references in order for the story to stay in the *present time*—you should do the same.

The action depicted in *SLUT* is intense and can be triggering. The characters in *SLUT* are in the midst of adolescence, and sex, drugs, and drinking often dominate their conversations. The humor, vulgarity, and insecurity displayed by the characters throughout the play must be a part of the conversation. While open to requests, no alteration of the script may be made without permission from Katie Cappiello.*

SLUT tells the story of eleven female characters. When considering casting, please note that the play makes most sense through the voice and eyes of teenage young women—actors of many races, ethnicities, and backgrounds have played each of these eleven characters. *SLUT* is one very specific story. This is essential to keep in mind during the conversation around the play and the culture of slut shaming it does or does not depict.

Finally, engaging your team in conversations about why you all are producing this show should be at the heart of your process. We encourage all involved to research the subject. Our suggestions are:

*Contact Katie with questions: Katie@TheArtsEffectNYC.com

- Jennifer Baumgardner's powerful documentary *It Was Rape* (also an invaluable preparation resource for your actors in *SLUT*)
- Producer Amy Ziering's award-winning film *The Invisible War*
- Black Women's Truth and Reconciliation Commission
- Leora Tanenbaum's *I Am Not a Slut: Slut-Shaming in the Age of the Internet*
- KnowYourIX.org
- The Anti-Violence Project

Consider building an advocacy campaign in conjunction with your production of *SLUT*. Find tips and resources at StopSlut.org. Most importantly, talk to students, classmates, parents, and friends about these issues and listen to their stories. Sexual shaming and violence touch everyone—give people a space to share, process, and heal.

Discussion Questions

Below you will find twenty-five questions to guide discussions around *SLUT*. These questions may be used in formal settings, such as a college or high school classrooms. They may also be used in informal settings, such as book club meetings, after-school programs and clubs, or even a get-together among friends.

1. In today's culture, what is a slut? Have you ever called someone a slut or been called a slut? When did you first hear this word? How has it shaped you and those in your community?

2. Throughout the play, Joey and the girls in her community grapple with universal conflicts. What are they? How are these challenges depicted in Joey's journey? How are they expressed through the other characters?

3. Do you empathize with some characters more than others? Consider not only the characters on

stage, but also characters we do not see (e.g., Jane's mom, Luke, George, and Tim). What do you think are the motivations driving the characters you found the least sympathetic?

4. How do Joey's actions influence her community's view of her before the incident in the cab and after? Was there a point in the play when your opinion of Joey changed? If so, what triggered this shift in perspective?

5. How and why are girls and women encouraged to lead with their sexuality? How are they socially rewarded for dressing provocatively and being sexually active? In what scenes are the characters struggling to negotiate sexual boundaries? How and why are they also shamed for doing so? Is the same true for all people, no matter the gender? If yes, how? If no, why?

6. The character Leila feels insecure about the fact that she and George have not had sex. How do "Virgin or Vamp" and "Prude or Slut" dichotomies impact the sexual development of young people?

7. In *SLUT*, what evidence do we see of a sexual double standard? Why do double standards exist in our society? Can you give examples of high-profile instances in recent months or years?

8. We watch the Slut Squad members try to own their sexuality by calling each other sluts. Have you

observed anyone successfully use the word slut in a positive way? Can it be a badge of honor? What are ways girls and women authentically own their sexuality? Why is that important?

9. Why do the Slut Squad members turn on Joey? Are they justified? Why do girls slut shame other girls?

10. What pressures are Luke, George, and Tim facing that influence their assault of Joey? What pressures do boys and young men face when it comes to exploring and expressing their sexual selves?

11. Can you understand Tim's decision to stay silent when he was in the cab? Why or why not? Do bystanders bear any responsibility to intervene in these types of situations? If you were Tim's sibling or parent what would you encourage him to do after the assault happened? What could Tim have done that would have protected him . . . and Joey? How can communities best prepare bystanders?

12. Gang mentality has an impact on the events depicted in the play. How? Why?

13. When Joey describes her rape, she details specific things said by George and Luke ("I feel like I'm wrestling an alligator or some shit.") and the cruel battle to make her orgasm. What is significant about how the boys seem to be performing this assault?

14. Jane struggles with and is disappointed by her mom's judgment and lack of support for Joey. What role do parents play in slut shaming? How can parents effectively support their teenage sons and daughters as they grow into their sexual selves? How can other adults—teachers, aunts, uncles, grandparents, neighbors, faith leaders, etc., be supportive and lend guidance?

15. In the play, we see Dominique processing the shame and embarrassment she feels as she attempts to acquire condoms—whether asking her mom, the nurse, or even simply purchasing them from a pharmacy. From where does this embarrassment and shame stem? What roles should schools and teachers play in engaging students in frank conversations about sex including the realities of sexual harassment and assault? What about parents? Media creators?

16. In *SLUT*, we find out that Tim, Luke, and George have been put on academic probation. Was this the appropriate disciplinary action taken by the school? What role should school administrators and teachers play in sexual assault cases when their students are involved?

17. What do you think of Joey's decision to press charges against Tim, Luke, and George? What factors led to Sylvie's decision not to press charges? Is it always the "right" decision to take legal action when you are a victim of sexual assault? Why or why not?

18. Why does Sylvie share her story with Joey? How does it impact Joey? Why is storytelling important? How can we cultivate ways in which people can share their stories with each other?

19. Both Joey and Sylvie contemplate what it means to consent. What is consent? Who carries the burden of consent? How can we shift the general understanding of consent in order to promote healthier, safer sexual interactions between partners?

20. How does the story SLUT change when it is set in a different neighborhood? When Joey's background changes? When she is of a different class? When she is of a different race?

21. How does the story SLUT change when any of the characters sexualities are changed? What if Joey were a different gender or had a different sexual orientation?

22. How does social media play a role in SLUT? How has the increased use of technology affected rape and sexual assault cases?

23. Female sexual shaming and rape are global problems. What examples can you give of how these issues manifest in other countries or cultures? What can we do to help increase awareness and commitment to stopping sexual assault and rape around the world?

24. What are things we all can do to help StopSlut?

25. What do you think happens after the final scene in the play? What does the future hold for each of the characters?

Slut in the Age of the Internet

LEORA TANENBAUM

At a time when insults travel at warp speed, calling a girl or woman a slut or ho in US youth culture has become prevalent, casual, and normalized—and there is not one single good thing that comes out of being called a slut or ho, even if your best friend is the one calling you this name, even if you're the one calling yourself this name.

Two decades ago, back in the prehistoric 1990s when there was no sexting, texting, instant messaging, Facebook bragging, or Snapchatting, I interviewed fifty girls and women who had been labeled sluts or hos in middle school or high school. Back then, the experience of being labeled a slut or ho was not rare, but it also was not ordinary. At that time, just about every middle school and high school seemed to have one, maybe two, girls designated a slut or ho at any given moment. Of course, that was one or two girls too many. The school slut was shamed, ostracized, physically harassed, pressured to have sex she didn't want, and raped. Those who mistreated her justified their actions on the grounds that the school slut was "too" sexual, and therefore deserved policing or punishment. In fact, in many cases she was not sexually active at all; when she was, she often wasn't any more so than her peers.

Two decades after completing my original research, I conducted a new set of interviews, speaking with fifty-five girls and women in the United States and Canada, most between the ages of fourteen and twenty-two, who had also been labeled sluts and hos. As with the girls and women I interviewed in the 1990s, they were diverse racially, economically, and geographically.

Their stories show that in many ways, the narrative of the slut is the same today as it ever was. Most of the time, the word continues to be used with the intent of shaming a girl or woman. Only girls and women are shamed, rarely boys and men, because of the sexual double standard—a bundle of sexist presuppositions that structure our behaviors. Yet today, sexual labeling operates differently from the way it used to.

I see three notable differences in today's usage of slut and ho. First, the Internet has made it easier than ever before for any girl or young woman to project and circulate a sexually sophisticated identity that bears no resemblance to her actual sexual experience (which may be nonexistent), and easier for others to respond by damaging her reputation. A generation ago, a sexually inexperienced girl who wanted to appear racy may have gone crazy with mascara and eye shadow, or hiked up her skirt after she left for school in the morning. Her parents generally knew who her friends were and when she was going out to see them. But today, a girl can take a photo of her naked breasts and Snapchat it to a guy she likes, or post a bikini shot on Facebook or Instagram, and her parents will probably have no idea that she has done so.

Meanwhile, bullies of yesteryear had to at least show their faces when they made life miserable for others. Even if they spray-painted "slut" on a girl's front porch one night or surreptitiously scratched "whore" onto her school locker, they had to make an effort that carried the risk of exposure. Today, anyone can be an anonymous bully with the touch of a finger on a slim, handheld gadget. It doesn't take guts to be a bully because you don't have to expose yourself and take responsibility for your actions. For the girl who is targeted, the experience of being labeled a slut is heightened and sharpened like never before. In today's electronic age, slut is an identity with no escape. It is part of a permanent digital record.

A second difference is that, unlike in previous generations, today the label snares nearly every young woman. All girls in middle school, high school, and even college can expect to be called a slut eventually, if they haven't been already. When I think back to the situation of two decades ago, when schools had only one or two girls whom others labeled as sluts, I am amazed; we should be so lucky today. Twenty years ago, mistreatment of the school slut, scary and sexist and sad, was at least not rampant. She stood out precisely because she was somewhat unusual.

Today, slut bashing goes far beyond bullying. The words slut and ho are heard everywhere—not only in school hallways and cafeterias. These words are heard in prime-time television shows, in music, in social media comments, in face-to-face conversations. Today, many girls and women refer to their social equals as "sluts." Sometimes this usage is casual and devoid of an intention to denigrate. Other times the name-caller is motivated to generate "drama"—to whip up public attention, to create excitement, to emulate the dynamics of reality television, in which life isn't worth living unless there's an antagonist to contend with. Sometimes this "drama" is hostile and cruel; it is meant to hurt, and it does.

In my research I distinguish between "slut bashing," which is a type of bullying, and "slut shaming," which is more diffuse. Slut bashing, I argue, is verbal harassment in which a girl is intentionally targeted because she doesn't adhere to feminine norms. Slut shaming, on the other hand, is the act of labeling someone a slut in a nonbullying context. It is a casual and often indirect form of judgment. It is everywhere. Regardless of intent, slut shaming is absolutely corrosive and wrong. Calling a girl or woman a slut, even in a seemingly benign context, ultimately results in policing not only of the specific female involved but of all females everywhere.

A third difference is that today many girls and women choose to label themselves as sluts—good sluts—to assert a positive, even defiant, attitude about their sexuality. As long as they control the label, many adolescent girls say that they enjoy the sexual attention they receive from their peers. To them, slut or slutty conveys a female who possesses sexual equality with males. If you're around a group of teenage girls or young women, you may hear them call out "Hey slut" to one another instead of "Hey girlfriend." However, it can be hard to know the intention of the speaker for sure. Sometimes in this context, slut is meant to be affectionate. But sometimes the intention is to police another girl, to warn her that she's being watched. The speaker herself may not even be clear about her own intent, or she may have dual goals—to be a vivacious friend and a guardian of sexual values.

Girls today believe that it's acceptable to ironically or playfully call themselves and their friends sluts or hos, and often they are rewarded with social approval. But just as often, there's a disconnect between their intentions and the consequences enacted by others, who may not be clued in to the irony and playfulness.

I recognize that some individual girls and women feel empowered when they call themselves and their friends sluts or hos on their own terms. Nevertheless, I question whether this usage is an effective feminist strategy when employed on a large scale. Repeatedly, girls and women tell me that they chose to call themselves sluts but subsequently lost control over the term when others then used the label against them. They used slut or ho to mean they were an empowered "good slut," but others turned around the word to mean that they were a shameful, promiscuous "bad slut." Despite its worthwhile intentions, reclaiming the word slut may end up causing more harm than good.

These three new elements in today's world—the Internet, the omnipresence of the label, and the phenomenon of young females choosing to call themselves sluts or hos—interlock to form a toxic environment for girls and young women.

We see these three elements dovetail with social media, which puts girls' and women's physical bodies perpetually on display. Many of us have come to believe that our bodies should always be visible and available. We judge other female bodies, and our female bodies are always judged. Today, we worry about our physical selves and sexual identities in a newly charged way. Performance and surveillance are now central to everyone's lives, and especially so for girls and young women.

Social media tantalizes us with the ability to control the way others see us. We create online profiles, upload photos and videos, and craft an identity we want others to admire. With every keystroke, we imagine that we are shaping our identity to project the best image and reputation possible. Yet the promise of controlling our image and reputation is false. Others take what we offer online and manipulate the raw material. We don't truly control our online identity.

It's no wonder that slut bashing and slut shaming have become commonplace. The stakes are higher than ever before in the performance of identity, and especially so for young females. If a girl wants to be socially relevant, she can't opt out of online performance (as if opting out really were possible in our digitally connected world). Maneuvering to become the center of attention as a "good slut" is the new normal, and judgment about other girls' sluttiness comes into play.

In short, the label "slut" is far more common, and utterly more confusing, than ever before. But one thing has not changed: regardless of context, the consequences of being labeled a slut or ho are nearly always damaging. Here are some of the ways this label can cause harm:

- These labels suggest to girls and women that their primary value comes from being sexually desirable and available. Yet paradoxically, slut and ho also signify that being sexually desirable and available reduce a female's worth. From every angle, females are evaluated through a sexual prism.

- Slut props up a rape culture in which many people, men and women alike, believe that coercing a female to perform sexual acts she doesn't want to do, or to which she can't say no, is unproblematic. If a girl or woman is sexually assaulted, she is said to deserve it because she's, well, a slut.

- It can lead girls and women to engage in self-destructive behaviors such as drug use and abuse, disordered eating, disordered sexual behavior, and suicide attempts.

- It compromises the sexual health of girls and women because they may feel inhibited from using contraceptives or even from making an appointment with a health-care provider, leading to unintended pregnancies and sexually transmitted diseases.

I believe that the best strategy to interrupt these

harmful dynamics is for all of us to stop using the word slut, even playfully. It's true that reclaiming the word may be a coping mechanism for some who have survived sexual violence or slut bashing. No one can control the fluidity of linguistic development, and the meanings of slut will shift over time organically. And yes, I recognize the humor in reclaiming slut, and I believe that feminist activism should be humorous and joyous. Nevertheless, I remain concerned that reclamation can trigger a terrible backlash against women.

I ask everyone to pause and consider the harm caused by this word. Let us recognize that no matter what a girl or woman has done sexually, no matter what clothes she wears, no matter what has happened to her, no matter what her body looks like, and no matter who she is, she never deserves to be labeled a slut.

Who Really Benefits from Slut Shaming?

DUANE de FOUR

Hello reader. I'm going to start off by asking you to do something for me. Don't worry, it's quick and easy and all you need is a pencil or pen. You won't even need to get up from your comfortable reading position. Ready? In the space below (or on a separate sheet of paper, or even in your head) I'd like you to take a minute and write down names you've heard for women who have sex:

Women:

All done? Okay, now I'd like you to use the space below (or on a separate sheet of paper, or brain space) to write down names you've heard for men who have sex:

Men:

That's it! Thank you for participating. Easy, right? I'd venture to guess that if you're anything like the thousands of participants who've done this activity with me before, your lists probably look something like these:

Women:
   Slut
   Whore
   Ho
   THOT (That Ho Over There)
   Loose
   Dirty
   Mattress
   Doorknob
   Prostitute
   Hooker
   (Oops! Ran out of space, but I could go on!)

Men:

Player/playa

Pimp

Stud

The man

Lucky

Dog

Man-whore

Like meat and potatoes and mom's apple pie, the names you see on these lists are what I like to call the American standards. And since there are a seemingly infinite number of regional and cultural variations of these words, you likely have some names on your lists that aren't on mine. I can tell you that I've facilitated this activity hundreds of times and without fail the most mentioned names are slut, ho, and whore for the women, and player and pimp for the men. These are the names participants are quick to yell out, sometimes reluctantly and sometimes with a frightening amount of pride and glee. (By the way, pat yourself on the back if "normal" or something similar made it on your lists. I'm proud of you.)

What I find amusing, and disturbing, about this activity is the way participants seem to quickly forget that their facilitator(s) simply ask for names for women (and later men) who have sex. I didn't ask you, for example, to come up with the most hurtful names you can think of. I didn't suggest a list of offensive names and I certainly never encouraged you to dig deep and get creative with the insults. Yet that's what facilitators always get, an expulsion of the most hurtful, offensive, and insulting words that participants know. But these aren't just random insults and hurtful names, they are the words and phrases that make up the heterosexist languages of slut shaming and victim blaming. Two languages that, sadly, seemingly everyone speaks.

Upon seeing these two lists side-by-side, many people first notice the huge tonal difference. The women's list is clearly more negative and derogatory than the men's list. Yet when this is pointed out at least one woman in the audience will always say, "Hey, wait a minute! I call my friends whores all the time and those skanks love it! They know I don't mean it offensively." While it's true that some women will occasionally call their female friends things like whore and skank in jest, or as a term of endearment, this does not remove the negative tone and purpose of these words in the larger social sphere. For example, a woman may laugh when her female friends jokingly call her a whore, but that doesn't make the word any less frightening when a random group of sexually aggressive men on a street corner calls her the same.

The same cannot be said for the names on the men's list. Player, pimp, stud, etc., are simply not fear inducing nor victim blaming. A man may dislike being called a player or a pimp by his friends, but rarely, if ever, will that man fear being harassed or assaulted when a woman or group of women calls him one. This isn't to say men don't get harassed and assaulted by women, just that this language doesn't generally coincide with such behavior. It's far more likely that he'd be called names from the women's list or other emasculating words. Additionally, it's all but guaranteed that even if a man doesn't like being called a player or pimp, a fair number of other men will view him with respect and maybe even jealousy, wondering just how much sex he's had to earn that reputation.

The power differential between the two lists should also be instantly apparent. The differential is easy to see when comparing two names, one from each list, that are closely related to one another: pimp and whore. A pimp and a whore are not equals. The pimp does what he wants with the whore and sells her body to others (or forces her to do it for him). Pimps are also violent and controlling. A fact so well known, that all one needs to say are the words "pimp slap" and almost everyone knows exactly what it means. It's no accident that on the female list we find whore and on the corresponding men's list we find pimp. This reality speaks directly to our cultural approach to sex and our views on male and female sexuality.

As Thomas MacAulay Millar argues in his essay "Toward a Performance Model of Sex," our current cultural view of sex is based on a commodity model. A heterosexist model that teaches women when they have sex, they lose something of value and therefore, engaging in "too much sex" will leave them valueless. Meanwhile, men are taught that they must, by any means necessary, obtain that precious commodity before "too many men" experience it and its value is lost. It should be clear after looking at these lists that the languages of slut shaming and victim blaming help to grease the wheels of this model and keep it running. The question then becomes, who really benefits from all this?

Certainly not women. They're forced to contend with a demented catch-22 when it comes to their sexuality. On the one hand, a woman who chooses not to have sex is called a prude (a term which comes with its own set of repercussions), and on the other she's a whore or a slut chipping away at her value. Either way, the choice of what to do with her body and sexuality is at least partially, if not totally, taken out of her hands.

Is it men who benefit, then? Somewhat, but to say men as a whole are the primary beneficiaries of the commodity model may be going a step too far. In the commodity model of sex, not only does men's sexuality lack any inherent value but men are also pushed to be in constant control, distant from each other and women, and in constant competition. There is a distinct advantage to being in control of course, but the expectation this creates for male behavior leads to its own share of trouble. The names in the list we discussed earlier give some indication of the problematic role this model creates for men.

Consider for a minute why "dog" often appears on the list of names for men who have sex. Any ideas why men are sometimes referred to as dogs? Here's a secret: It's not because like a real dog, men are stereotyped to be loyal, loving, and affectionate. No, it's a reference to the stereotype of men acting like dogs in heat, led solely by their penises, not their brains. What's being implied when a man is called a dog, is that he can't control his urges, can't control his sexuality, and can't control himself around women. More so than any other name on the male list, the name dog is meant as an insult, generally used only when a man cheats or engages in other hurtful acts. It's odd, then, that men are compared to dogs even when it's not meant as an insult, but a defense of certain male behaviors around women. No matter how the name or the comparison is used, it implies the same thing: men can't control their sexual urges.

The harmful and rape-perpetuating impact of this belief should be self-evident. Assuming men can't control their sexuality enables society to give men a "Get Out of Jail Free" card, a pass to commit sexual harassment, assault, and rape with the ready-made excuse, "I couldn't control myself." I can't tell you how many times I've heard people make statements along the lines of: "When a woman wears revealing clothing around a man it's like holding a juicy steak in front of a dog. He can't stop himself from staring, saying something, or touching." So not only are we calling men "brainless animals" and women "meat," we're also victim blaming. It makes no sense and it also assumes that even if men managed to keep their urges in check, all men inherently desire to comment on, stare at, or touch random women on the street.

In defense of real dogs, I'd like to point out something else that always bothers me about this comparison. My dog loves steak as much as any other dog, but she's also well behaved. I leave food within her reach all the time and I promise you, no matter how much she wants to, she won't eat it unless I tell her it's okay to do so. Like dogs, humans (yes, even male humans) grow up learning that living in a civilized and sanitary society requires us to control many of our urges until they are appropriate to indulge.

The contradiction here is, at the same time men are being told they can't control their sexuality, they're also being taught to exert control over those with whom they want to have sex. A pimp controls "his" hos, so for a man to emulate a pimp he must exert control over those with whom he's having sex. Meanwhile, a player maintains control of his partners through deception and trickery. Both these models of masculinity exist solely as a result of the commodity model of sex. Their goal is to control or manipulate women and obtain their value as commodities. Or to put it more correctly, obtain the commodity from women who, in this model, are nothing more than gatekeepers. But let's be clear about something: this dominance imperative isn't merely a suggestion. Men are very much pushed into this role—by choice or by force. When a man doesn't fulfill his assigned role, he's ridiculed, called names, ostracized, and sometimes punished with physical violence.

This belief that men are always in charge and in control sexually leads many men to deny experiences of rape or sexual assault, whether the perpetrator is female or male. Which explains another frequent experience I have during trainings: situations where men share stories that are clearly sexual assaults they've experienced, but then deny because, "men can't be raped." (This statement never ceases to blow my mind.) Another version of this is the men who reframe their stories of assault as moments of male empowerment, or youthful vigor, which tends to happen when the story involves a boy being assaulted by an older girl or woman.

Musicians Chris Brown and Lil Wayne are perfect examples of this phenomenon. Brown revealed in an interview that at age eight he "had sex" with a girl age fourteen or fifteen. But in his telling of the story he was already "hot to trot" and unafraid to talk to women. Adding to the hypermasculine framing of the event, this early experience made him, in his words, "a beast" and "the best" in bed. Lil Wayne on the other hand has gone into graphic detail of his assault at age eleven by a girl who was thirteen. Yet despite revealing that he was tricked into the situation, and that he tried to push the girl off before finally giving in and letting her "do what she do" he doesn't call his experience rape (and apparently neither does anyone around him). This is what cognitive dissonance looks like.

Fearing how they'll be perceived, male survivors of rape and assault are less likely to report it than women. Male survivors frequently blame themselves as well, questioning why they weren't "strong enough" or "dominant enough" to prevent the rape from happening. In the heteronormative commodity model of sex, rape is a naturally occurring by-product of one group (women) holding all the valuable tickets that men want to get their hands on. As Millar argues, it therefore amounts to nothing more than a property crime (which explains why survivors have been so poorly treated in our society). But in that same model, there's no framework for understanding the rape of men, whether the perpetrator is male or female. If male sexuality has no inherent value, why would anyone want to take it by force or coercion? Thus, male survivors who view sex and sexuality through this lens lack the framework to understand what happened to them, and why.

This brings us to the one and only group of people who truly benefit from these cultural norms—perpetrators of sexual violence. No matter the gender of the perpetrator, they are without a doubt the only group of people truly benefiting from our current cultural norms around sex, slut shaming, and victim blaming. Even worse, they are masters at using this terrible trifecta to both aid them in committing assaults and cover them up afterward.

The work of Dr. David Lisak, a researcher who studied men who had committed rape but were never caught (who he calls undetected rapists), will prove most helpful here. He learned that these undetected rapists were able to commit multiple assaults without ever getting caught (an average of six assaults each at the time of his research). He also learned how they were able to offend so frequently by interviewing a number of them to learn their tactics in great detail. Again, one of his key findings was the discovery of how these cultural norms play right into perpetrators' hands.

Figuring out how these guys work shouldn't be

too difficult to guess at this point. First off, who do you think would be a more successful rapist, a creepy-looking guy who wears hoodies all the time, drives a creepy windowless van, and talks and acts like a horror-movie villain, or the guy who looks and acts just like his peers? The second one, of course, because no one will suspect him. But that's just the start.

Perpetrators identify their victims, who they call targets, then maneuver them into positions of vulnerability and isolation. This is what Dr. Lisak describes as grooming. In the grooming process, the perpetrator establishes himself as a good guy who the target begins to trust. He's also building trust with the target's friends (if they're around) and framing things in a way that suits his purposes. In other words, establishing his alibi. Okay, here's another question for you. If he disguises himself as a normal guy that means he has friends. So, how do you think his friends see him? As "Frank, my rapist friend" or "Frank, my friend who's a total pimp! The dude who gets laid all the time!"

What about his target, any guesses what picture he's painting of her? That's right. She's a "slutty girl who just wants to get laid" or she's "totally into him and down to fuck." If they're in a bar or at a party he's also getting her intoxicated. Basically, he's laying the groundwork for the slut shaming he'll be doing later. Finally he creates situations where he is able to get her alone and isolated. Things like, "Oh, I'll take her home" or "I'll look out for her" or "Come over and let's study together." Whatever it is, the picture has been painted in everyone else's mind that he's a good guy who would never hurt anyone, and she's into him, or she's totally slutty. Then when they're alone with no witnesses, he commits his assault, making sure not to hurt her in any other way that might be used as evidence against him later (beyond the rape, of course, which he can claim was just consensual sex).

After the assault, the victim blaming and slut shaming continues. "She was so slutty. She was dirty. You won't believe the things she let me do to her!" Most don't question this because the situation looked just like it was supposed to—a player working his magic and a girl "ready to give it up." It played out just like any other hookup and *besides, there were no signs of violence and he doesn't deny they had sex and no one believes that he's the kind of guy who would do such a thing and she's just a whore who had sex with all these men before therefore she can't be trusted and she's not a virgin what a slut and she wanted it she's just regretting her choice because she doesn't want to be seen as a slut and she's lying she just wants some of his money or a piece of his fame and he can get any girl he wants why would he rape her and she was wearing a short skirt and she went up to his room at 2 a.m. and she was drunk and acting like a slut.* Any of that sound familiar? The commodity model of sex mixed with slut shaming and victim blaming with all three working to the benefit of this rapist. The end result? This:

Due to a lack of research, far less is known about female perpetrators of rape and sexual assault. We

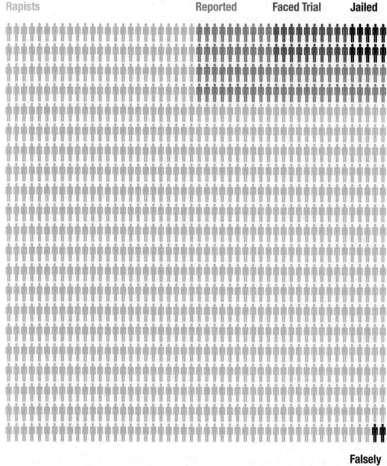

Rapists Reported Faced Trial Jailed

Falsely
Accused

Image courtesy of The Enliven Project: The Truth about False
Accusation.

do know that women tend to use power differentials to their advantage (age, status, wealth) when committing assaults but little else. But is it hard to imagine them using similar tactics? Again, I have no empirical evidence to support this, but based on my twenty years of experience in the rape prevention field and the anecdotal evidence I've encountered in that time, I have some theories. My guess is that one of the main differences is instead of relying on slut shaming, female perpetrators can rely on cultural beliefs that women don't rape (other women or men) and men can't be raped (because any real man always wants to have sex) to effectively cover their crimes.

Take the case of Florida middle school teacher Debra LaFave: LaFave, who was twenty-five at the time, raped one of her fourteen-year-old male students and served no jail time (although she was put under house arrest). Reporting around the case rarely used the word "rape." Instead, there was lots of "had sex with," additionally, much of the reporting focused on her looks. Her lawyer called her "too pretty for prison" and a book was even written—by her husband—with the title *Gorgeous Disaster*. Beyond the reporting, in much of the dialogue around the case, the fourteen-year-old boy was called "lucky." So in the commodity model of sex, even when a boy is raped by an adult woman, he's perceived to be not a victim, but rather a winner.

In the end, the question we have to ask is: Who benefits from slut shaming? Who benefits when we spend our energy looking into a victim's/accuser's/complainant's/survivor's past and not the perpetrator's/respondent's/defendant's past? Who benefits when we ask questions such as "Why was she there?" "Why did she drink so much?" "Why did she walk home with him?" "Why was she wearing that short skirt?" and not, "Why did he rape her?" Who benefits when all our attention is on the victim and not the perpetrator? The perpetrator, that's who benefits. This is how perpetrators are able to be so proficient. They know how to use the commodity model of sex, slut shaming, and victim blaming to their advantage and we allow them to do it. We are complicit in their crimes.

And another perpetrator gets away, ready and willing to assault again.

My Story
Shaming and Assault in the Queer Community

JOHN KELLY

Writing down my experiences and what I have learned and what I hope to pass on is always a greater challenge than anticipated. My name is John Kelly, I am a survivor of rape and intimate-partner violence, and I'm queer. There. I said it—that's the hard part.

I came to college at Tufts University in suburban Medford, Massachusetts, unsuspecting, eager, and questioning my sexuality. Early on, a queer student who was three years older than I began to take an interest in me, and by around March of my first year we were dating. Soon after that, the abuse began. It started off innocuously enough—just a put-down here, a backhanded compliment there. Before long, it became more controlling; there were threats to end the relationship and spread rumors about me, restrictions of where I could and couldn't go, and requirements that I be ready to see him at the drop of a hat and ready for him to leave whenever he chose. The combination of his erratic behavior with intense restrictions on what I could do left me paralyzed. This was the first guy who ever expressed interest in me—I had only recently realized my identity as queer, so I was new to that scene. When would be the next time a guy liked me? I had one here who did, so why mess with that? Since he was the first, he set the bar for what I thought I deserved and how I saw myself being treated in a relationship.

Finally, the last night of my first year rolled around. We were still together, in what I thought at the time was just a normal relationship. Sure, my partner was mean to me, shouted at me, and controlled most of my life, but he said he liked me! We had agreed to take a break for the summer, since we wouldn't be in the same location, and then see where we stood when we both came back from our summer vacations. Wait, actually, hold on. We didn't make that decision; he did. Then, on our last night together, he held me down and raped me, while I cried and said no. I didn't see it as rape back then, because we were dating, and I'm queer and male-bodied, and I had never heard a narrative like mine, so I thought it must just not happen. "He has needs," I told myself. During the rape, he said, "I love you," for the first time.

Immediately after the assault ended, he told me to leave. Confused, shaken, and hurt by his actions already, I now felt the sting of rejection—it was our last night together, and we had agreed to spend it together. I had even packed up my entire dorm room, so not even my sheets were still on the bed, which he knew and had encouraged. He wouldn't talk, so finally, in tears, I tried to leave. As I stood up to leave, he asked if I loved him, and I told him I couldn't say that to him. At this point, he grabbed my wrist forcefully, telling me he wouldn't let go until I told him I loved him, and promised to come see him the next morning before I left. I tried to pull away, to get out, to just leave, but I couldn't get him off me. Finally, I gave in. "I love you," I said. He let me go, I saw him the next morning, and said it again.

Abuse doesn't always stop when a relationship ends. He had some of my belongings, which I asked him to mail to me. He told me he wouldn't because they "reminded him of me." He would tell me we couldn't speak to each other, only to reach out to me in a fit over something he heard about me doing. I didn't want anything to do with him, but his control of me hadn't ended. I started seeing someone else, though when I talked to her about my past relationship, I didn't hint at the abuse because I myself was still running from it.

Finally, I was back at school for my sophomore year, ready to start fresh. The first week back, celebrations with friends got too rowdy and before I knew it I had blacked out. From what I've been able to piece together from witnesses' accounts, my RA found me stumbling and vomiting, and asked me to call someone to take care of me. I called the only person who had taken care of me before and was already on campus—my abusive ex. I came to as I was screaming at him in my bedroom; my RA tells me she heard him having sex with me—no, not with me, but on me—from her room next door, and came over to stop it because she knew how drunk I was. The kicker? She had told my ex the same thing when she let him into my building—that I was too drunk to do anything that night. It didn't stop him, and to this day I still don't really know what happened that night. But one thing is clear from his account of the events—he raped me.

Not remembering has its benefits and dire implications. I get terrified if I'm not in control, and occasionally I get snapshots from that night that I've never seen before. One thing I do remember is the feeling—a sinking, broken, hurt, confused, gut-wrenching feeling.

Slowly, I began to piece together my history of abuse. It took me over a year before I truly came to terms with the level of abuse that I experienced. I reported my assailant to the university, which found him responsible, and suspended him for a year. I have it so, so much better than many college survivors, who either cannot come forward to report or see lesser—if any—punishments handed down. I dealt with his impending return for the next year, until eventually he chose to withdraw completely from Tufts after another unrelated investigation.

The investigation took an entire semester, during which my assailant remained on campus and went about life as normal. This is something that often doesn't receive press attention—how do you live with your abuser or rapist down the street? At first I tried to just continue living as I had during the year he was gone. But one night I was at a friend's party, and he showed up. I immediately left in a panic. Later that night, I attempted suicide. I ended up spending five days in a mental hospital, which were the only five days I had without fear of seeing him. When

I returned to school, I didn't socialize, the dining halls and walks to class became living nightmares, and god knows I couldn't go to parties. My grades suffered and panic attacks became a daily reality. Once his suspension began, I reclaimed some sense of safety, but I don't think I will ever feel the same safety as I did before the abuse. No, he never came out of the bushes to attack me, but if I feel someone walking behind me my heart jumps up into my throat—I worry it's him.

Since then, I've had the incredible opportunity to become an activist against campus sexual assault, especially against sexual violence in the queer community. I've been on MSNBC, NPR, CNN, Feministing, Jezebel, and other media outlets. I testified before the US Senate, becoming the first person to testify about same-sex dating violence in the history of Congress. These experiences have been incredibly influential in my own personal healing process. I try to use my platform to spread greater knowledge about queer sexual and intimate-partner violence, with the hope that some day queer folks' experiences won't be questioned, and justice will be achieved for those still suffering.

The Facts

It cannot be disputed that men are far and above the primary perpetrators of sexual violence. The 2010 National Intimate Partner and Sexual Violence Survey (NISVS) shows that 98 percent of female rape victims and 93 percent of male rape victims report having only male perpetrators.[1] It is important to note, however, that the same gender norms that allow men to rape at such staggering rates also create ideals of masculinity that silence male survivors. The number of male survivors is higher than generally understood, particularly among at-risk demographics such as queer and gender-nonconforming men. The NISVS showed that one in seventy-one men are victims of rape (forced oral or anal penetration), and nearly one in five men experience some other form of sexual violence (such as the 5 percent of men who have been forced to penetrate someone else.)

While female perpetration is rare, it does occur against men and against women. Violence can occur regardless of sexual orientation, which means that straight men can be sexually assaulted by other straight men, or by a queer-identified male. A queer-identified male can be assaulted by a straight male, or by another queer male, or by a woman. While these different forms of violence occur at different rates, it's important to remember that behind these statistics are people who have stories, and every single story is just as legitimate as the next. The people perpetrating this violence are most often people you already know, although occasionally strangers perpetrate these assaults.

Any conversation about sexual assault is lacking if attention is not paid to those groups with high

1. Black, M.C. et al (2011). *The National Intimate Partner and Sexual Violence Survey (NISVS): 2010 Summary Report.* Atlanta, GA: National Center for Injury Prevention and Control, Centers for Disease Control and Prevention.

rates of sexual violence. Women of color, queer people, trans* people, and disabled people all experience sexual victimization at higher rates than the rest of the population, and attention must be paid to them. For queer folks, "the median estimate of lifetime sexual assault for GB [Gay or Bisexual] men was 30 percent and the median estimate of lifetime sexual assault for LB [Lesbian or Bisexual] women was 43 percent . . . LGB individuals may be at increased risk for sexual assault victimization."[2] In terms of queer relationships, rates of domestic and dating violence are also incredibly high: "Between 25 and 33 percent of all same-sex relationships have been involved in domestic violence."[3] The higher rates of victimization are compounded by the mistreatment these populations historically have experienced by society at large and specifically by the criminal justice system, something that also will contribute to lower rates of reporting. Indeed, "The intersection of factors such as gender, class, ethnicity, and previous victimization history may generate a pattern of harm and recovery that is more intricate than what has been accounted for in most literature on trauma."[4]

2. Emily F. Rothman, Deinera Exner, and Allyson L. Baughman. "The Prevalence of Sexual Assault Against People Who Identify as Gay, Lesbian, or Bisexual in the United States: A Systematic Review," Trauma, Violence, & Abuse 12, no. 2 (2011): 55–66, doi:10.1177/1524838010390707.
3. Laura C. Booker and Sarah Jane Dodd, "Social Work Practice with Lesbian Couples," in Social Work Practice with Lesbian, Gay, Bisexual, and Transgender People, ed. Gerald P. Mallon, 2nd ed. (New York: Haworth, 2008): 179–99.
4. Sharon M. Wasco, "Conceptualizing the Harm Done by Rape: Applications of Trauma Theory to Experiences of Sexual Assault," Trauma, Violence, & Abuse 4, no. 4 (2003): 309–22, doi:10.1177/1524838003256560.

On Queerness, Maleness, Making Changes, and Reporting (Or Not)

Paying special attention to the needs of marginalized groups is important to acknowledging the effects insidious trauma has on these individuals. Insidious trauma "is usually associated with the devaluing of an individual's social status because of a characteristic of their identity. . . . Exposure to insidious trauma may lead individuals to conclude that an unchangeable aspect of their identity justifies their unequal worth and lack of protection from danger."[5] Society at large has a history of denigrating queer people, from homophobic sodomy and sexual violence laws that don't acknowledge or protect queer people, to the criminalization of HIV, to hate crimes experienced by the community as a whole and especially among trans* folks. This depreciation leads many queer people to experience insidious trauma, simply as a result of their sexuality. Insidious trauma, when coupled with an instantiation of sexual violence, has the terrifying ability to wreck the foundations of a queer person's sense of self. There is a duty to give extra care and time to such populations that experience such compounded traumas—to give voice to those so often and painfully silenced.

Same-sex sexual violence is something that has become more present in conversations around sexual assault, although popular culture and media portrayals of survivorship is still gendered in a way that often excludes queer survivors. Male-male sexual violence among adult populations brings with it

5. Ibid, 315.

a unique set of challenges and factors. This form of violence is most commonplace in gender-segregated communities, specifically institutions such as the military, fraternities and sports teams, the prison system, and among queer populations perpetrated by other queer men or by straight men. Sexual violence is always about power and not necessarily tied to sexual desire or preferences. Among male survivors who were victimized by other males, issues of masculinity and homophobia, either internalized or externalized, play into the roles and tropes of male survivors. These tropes thus impact the healing of those affected by this violence in a feedback loop that also contributes to the serious underreporting of male-male sexual violence.

It is often assumed that those who identify as male always want to have sex, especially those who identify as queer. According to this stereotype, men are always thinking about sex and thus always must be ready and willing to have sex. This simply is not the case. Whatever the stereotypes, desires vary, by person and by situation. Regardless of the reasons one has for not wanting sex, it is a choice that must be respected, regardless of gender, and regardless of what *Cosmo*, sitcoms, and movies may want us to believe. The stereotype may be comforting to some because it allows them to ignore the reality of sexual violence, but know that it is wrong. Men do not always want to have sex.

I've had close friends and family members ask, "Why didn't you just fight him off?" Whether or not someone attempts to stave off an act of sexual violence is not the same question as whether or not the sex was consensual. Additionally, any type of coercion—physical, emotional, economic—can make "fighting back" far from a viable option: assault may be facilitated by the power differentials within a romantic relationship, between a pledge and a fraternity brother, between a student and their professor, or because of size or age difference. Alcohol- or drug-induced assaults can occur regardless of one's real or perceived gender identity and/or expression.

Being a survivor does not make a person weak; not fighting someone off does not either. This narrative is based on gender norms that are socially constructed. In our society, there is an attitude that one's experience of violence is only legitimate if they fight back. Society teaches women, queer people, and other groups that fighting back isn't in their nature, and is a sign of a tendency toward violence or instability or undesirability. If this is something you've felt, don't worry, so have I. It is important to keep reminding ourselves that it simply isn't true. The fact that we continue to survive is a testament to our strength.

Another barrier to receiving care is often caused by the belief that the pain being experienced by the victim does not reach the level worthy of receiving care, especially when dealing with dating violence: "Date rapes and rapes by men who have had prior relationships with their victims also contain elements of coercive authority that militates against decisive resistance. Here the 'authority' takes the form of expected behavior."[6] Force is about more

6. Susan Brownmiller, *Against Our Will: Men, Women and Rape.* (New York: Simon and Schuster, 1975), 257.

than holding someone down—it is about trapping someone in a pattern, about an assumption of consent in a relationship, about an unspoken threat if a person is to say "no." Indeed, an often-cited issue is that assaults that don't result in broken bones, bruises, scars, or hospital visits must not be "violent enough" to necessitate help. However, "although many sexual assaults may include hallmark characteristics of trauma such as violence, injury, and fear of death, not all rapes do. For example, the National Violence Against Women Survey found that "up to 69 percent of rapes do not result in physical injury"[7]—that is over two-thirds of all assaults.

Something to never forget: physical arousal does not equal consent. For some male-bodied people, visible arousal may occur during an assault, and may lead to questioning by others or by oneself about the legitimacy of the violence. However, that is simply a body's way of reacting to stress and to a heightened state of awareness—nothing more, nothing else. Sometimes, ejaculation occurs, and this again does not equal consent in any way. A bodily reaction is not a "yes."

Ideas of masculinity may make you wonder if what happened to you was "really" assault (or rape, or nonconsensual, or "that thing," or any other words that feel best for you). That's okay, and because it is your experience, you get to call it whatever you want. You can call it one thing out loud and another thing in your head, and doubting it one day (or week or month or year) does not mean it did not happen.

7. Wasco, 312.

Indeed, in some cases people are able to hide experiences from themselves or from others for years, and that doesn't change what happened. If you experience doubt, know that you are by no means the only one, and it's an instinct that's ingrained in us. Admitting something traumatic happened to you is a challenging and difficult thing to do, and goes against what society has taught us about what it means to be human.

As a survivor and a queer person, it's hard to find narratives that represent our experiences. Media and pop culture most often choose to portray straight, cisgendered, white, female survivors, especially when the assailant is a stranger or at the very least not an intimate partner. In addition, assailants are often portrayed as black males, with large and intimidating figures, in dark alleys and behind bushes. However, that is not consistent with the full reality of sexual violence faced. When we don't see our own stories reflected in media, it leads to doubt. I didn't know queer relationships could be abusive, or that a queer person could be raped—I had never heard of it outside the context of prisons in any way, until I had my own experiences. I had no reassurance from society that my experience and pain was valid.

The question then becomes, "Where do we go from here?" in terms of our own healing and any desire we have to change culture. The answers to these questions are by no means simple, nor are they the same for every person. For me, going to therapy, sharing my story, and practicing my spirituality have all been undeniably helpful for my healing journey. My only advice is to do what feels most right—if you want to share your story with others, please do. Know that people will listen and people will care. Yes, occasionally you'll get a not-so-great response, and that is heartbreaking, but in my experience that has very much been the exception and by no means the rule. However, "going public" is not possible for everyone, either by circumstance or by choice. This in no way invalidates your experiences.

The same goes for reporting what has happened to you—to police, to your school, or to your work place. Under federal law you have the right to a workplace and school free from gender discrimination—that means an environment free from sexual harassment and sexual violence. For the workplace, this law is known as Title VII; for schools that receive federal funding this is Title IX. Under both of these laws, your sex, gender, and gender identity do not preclude you from this protection—they apply equally to trans* people and cis people, men and women. If something does happen to you, federal law protects you, and your institution must work to ensure your safety and ability to function. Not every state has laws that cover same-sex assaults or assaults perpetrated by women, so if you choose to go through the criminal justice system, it is important to double-check the laws of your state. However, reporting is not right for every person, and it is not up to anyone else but yourself to decide the best course for you.

Sexual violence happens, and it can happen to anyone. It happens to women and men, to straight and queer people, to those who conform to gender norms and to those of us who don't. It happened to me, and it might have happened to you, too. Healing is an ongoing process, and is by no means linear—there are good days and bad days, two-steps-forward-then-five-steps-back weeks and months, and there was even almost one whole day when I didn't think about my abuser or the abuse itself.

No matter your identity, you are not alone—please, remember that always.

An Open Letter from Black Women to the SlutWalk

FARAH TANIS

Black Women's Blueprint is a national, Black feminist organization using civil and human rights approaches to organize and develop a culture where women of African descent are fully empowered and where gender, race, and other disparities are erased. The organization engages in progressive research, historical documentation, and policy advocacy and is the convener of the first Truth Commission ever to focus on Black women in the United States and their historical and contemporary experiences with sexual assault.

The following letter was originally posted by Black Women's Blueprint on blackwomensblueprint.org on September 23, 2011, in advance of the New York City SlutWalk. It was widely read and discussed, and was signed by hundreds of supporters.

We the undersigned women of African descent and antiviolence advocates, activists, scholars, organizational and spiritual leaders wish to address the SlutWalk. First, we commend the organizers on their bold and vast mobilization to end the shaming and blaming of sexual assault victims for violence committed against them by other members of society. We are proud to be living in this moment in time where girls and boys have the opportunity to witness the acts of extraordinary women resisting oppression and challenging the myths that feed rape culture everywhere.

The police officer's comments in Toronto that ignited the organizing of the first SlutWalk and served to trivialize, omit, and dismiss women's continuous experiences of sexual exploitation, assault, and oppression are an attack on our collective spirits. Whether the dismissal of rape and other violations of a woman's body be driven by her mode of dress, line of work, level of intoxication, her class, and in cases of Black and brown bodies—her race— we are in full agreement that no one deserves to be raped.

The Issue At Hand

We are deeply concerned. As Black women and girls we find no space in SlutWalk, no space for participation and to unequivocally denounce rape and sexual assault as we have experienced it. We are perplexed by the use of the term "slut" and by any implication that this word, much like the word "Ho" or the "N" word should be reappropriated. The way in which we are perceived and what happens to us before, during, and after sexual assault crosses the boundaries of our mode of dress. Much of this is tied to our particular history. In the United States, where slavery constructed Black female sexualities, Jim Crow kidnappings, rape and lynchings, gender misrepresentations, and more recently, where the Black female immigrant struggle combine, "slut" has different associations for Black women. We do not recognize ourselves nor do we see our lived experiences reflected within SlutWalk and especially not in its brand and its label.

As Black women, we do not have the privilege or the space to call ourselves "slut" without validating the already historically entrenched ideology and recurring messages about what and who the Black woman is. We don't have the privilege to play on destructive representations burned in our collective minds, on our bodies and souls for generations. Although we understand the valid impetus behind the use of the word "slut" as language to frame and brand an antirape movement, we are gravely concerned. For us the trivialization of rape and the absence of justice are viciously intertwined with narratives of sexual surveillance, legal access, and availability to our personhood. It is tied to institutionalized ideology about our bodies as sexualized objects of property, as spectacles of sexuality and deviant sexual desire. It is tied to notions about our clothed or unclothed bodies as unable to be raped whether on the auction block, in the fields, or on living room television screens. The perception and wholesale acceptance of speculations about what the Black woman wants, what she needs, and what she deserves has truly, long crossed the boundaries of her mode of dress.

We know the SlutWalk is a call to action and we have heard you. Yet we struggle with the decision to answer this call by joining with or supporting something that even in name exemplifies the ways in which mainstream women's movements have repeatedly excluded Black women even in spaces where our participation is most critical. We are still struggling with the how, why, and when, and ask at what impasse should the SlutWalk have included substantial representation of Black women in the building and branding of this US-based movement to challenge rape culture?

Black women have worked tirelessly since the nineteenth century colored women's clubs to rid society of the sexist and racist vernacular of slut, jezebel, hottentot, mammy, mule, sapphire; to build our sense of selves and redefine what women who look like us represent. Although we vehemently support a woman's right to wear whatever she wants anytime, anywhere, within the context of a "Slut-Walk" we don't have the privilege to walk through the streets of New York City, Detroit, DC, Atlanta, Chicago, Miami, LA, etc., either half-naked or fully clothed self-identifying as "sluts" and think that this will make women safer in our communities an hour later, a month later, or a year later. Moreover, we are careful not to set a precedent for our young girls by giving them the message that we can self-identify as "sluts" when we're still working to annihilate the word "ho," which deriving from the word "hooker" or "whore," as in "Jezebel whore" was meant to dehumanize. Lastly, we do not want to encourage our young men, our Black fathers, sons, and brothers to reinforce Black women's identities as "sluts" by normalizing the term on t-shirts, buttons, flyers, and pamphlets.

The personal is political. For us, the problem of trivialized rape and the absence of justice are intertwined with race, gender, sexuality, poverty, immigration, and community. As Black women in America, we are careful not to forget this or we may compromise more than we are able to recover. Even if only in name, we cannot afford to label ourselves, to claim identity, to chant dehumanizing rhetoric against ourselves in any movement. We can learn from successful movements like the Civil Rights movement, from Women's Suffrage, the Black Nationalist, and Black Feminist movements that we can make change without resorting to the taking back of words that were never ours to begin with, but in fact heaved upon us in a process of dehumanization and devaluation.

What We Ask

Sisters from Toronto, rape and sexual assault is a radical weapon of oppression and we are in full agreement that it requires radical people and radical strategies to counter it. In that spirit, and because there is so much work to be done and great potential to do it together, we ask that the SlutWalk be even more radical and break from what has historically been the erasure of Black women and their particular needs, their struggles as well as their potential and contributions to feminist movements and all other movements.

Women in the United States are racially and ethnically diverse. Every tactic to gain civil and human rights must not only consult and consider women of color, but it must equally center all our experiences and our communities in the construction, launching, delivery, and sustainment of that movement.

We ask that SlutWalk take critical steps to become cognizant of the histories of people of color and engage women of color in ways that respect culture, language, and context.

We ask that SlutWalk consider engaging in a rebranding and relabeling process and believe that given the current popularity of the Walk, its thousands of followers will not abandon the movement simply because it has changed its label.

We ask that the organizers participating in the SlutWalk take further action to end the trivialization of rape at every level of society. Take action to end the use of the word "rape" as if it were a metaphor and also take action to end the use of language invented to perpetuate racist and sexist structures and intended to dehumanize and devalue.

In the spirit of building a revolutionary movement to end sexual assault, end rape myths, and end rape culture, we ask that SlutWalk move forward in true authenticity and solidarity to organize beyond the marches and demonstrations as SlutWalk. Develop a more critical, a more strategic and sustainable plan for bringing women together to demand countries, communities, families, and individuals uphold each other's human right to bodily integrity and collectively speak a resounding NO to violence against women.

We would welcome a meeting with the organizers of SlutWalk to discuss the intrinsic potential in its global reach and the sheer number of followers it has energized. We'd welcome the opportunity to engage in critical conversation with the organizers of SlutWalk about strategies for remaining accountable to the thousands of women and men, marchers it left behind in Brazil, in New Delhi, South Korea, and elsewhere—marchers who continue to need safety and resources, marchers who went back home to their communities and their lives. We would welcome a conversation about the work ahead and how this can be done together with groups across various boundaries, to end sexual assault beyond the marches.

As women of color standing at the intersection of race, gender, sexuality, class, and more, we will continue to be relentless in the struggle to dismantle the unacceptable systems of oppression that designedly besiege our everyday lives. We will continue to fight for the development of policies and initiatives that prioritize the primary prevention of sexual assault, respect women and individual rights, agency, and freedoms, and hold offenders accountable. We will consistently demand justice whether under governmental law, at community levels, or via community strategies for those who have been assaulted; and organize to end sexual assaults of persons from all walks of life, all genders, all sexualities, all races, all ethnicities, and all histories.

Slut on the Latina Body

VERONICA ARREOLA

The word slut looks different on a Latina body. One might even say that slut is our default and that it takes a lot of work to remove.

I was labeled a slut in high school, in part, because I wore revealing clothing and was at ease with the art of flirting. While I sometimes hated my body because I thought I was fat, I knew the power it held. I also enjoyed the power that came with a low-cut paisley dress and combat boots. It's funny, I do not recall being aware of riot grrrl until college, but in high school I married hip-hop wear with grunge for my own riot grrrl style. I didn't know to label it feminist. Meanwhile, the girls who always dressed modestly, despite having sex with their boyfriends, called me a slut, something evil. I once had a boyfriend break up with me because his mom did not want him to date a girl "like me." I could only assume "like me" meant Latina and working class. The message was clear: I was dangerous for her son.

The teenage years are awkward enough with all the hormones a-raging and body parts a-changing, but throw in the Latina-sexpot layer on top of it and sometimes I am dumbfounded I survived high school at all.

My daughter is eleven and so far her body is following the same path mine did. As she is maturing my husband notices grown men giving her a double take. The first look says, "Oh, baby . . ." The second says, "Shit! That's a kid!" Thankfully, from what she reports, she has not received the harassment I endured at that age. Most notably, she hasn't experienced the boy in seventh-grade math who made sound effects (the bouncing of springs—*boing, boing*) as I walked into class.

Because of my own experiences, we had "the talk" years ago. And of course, I mean we *started* the talk about sex and sexuality because it never really ends. We began with the basics: how babies are made. Then on to how her body would be changing. I was inspired to have a conversation about sexual assault after she was assigned Maya Angelou for the school history fair. Maya was raped at a young age and then stopped speaking after the rapist was killed by her relatives. This rape is such a pivotal part of her story that it was even included in her biography intended for children. I sat with my daughter to explain this four-letter word and why the cascade of traumas caused by sexual violence made Maya stop talking.

The next time we had to talk about rape was after I took her to see *Divergent,* based on the best-selling YA dystopian series by Veronica Roth. She hadn't read the book yet; I had. I had forgotten that one of the fears of the main character, Tris, is having sex with Four, her combat trainer. In the book, it was a

SLUT ON THE LATINA BODY

natural fear—of intimacy and of having sex for the first time. The movie portrayed this anxiety not just as a fear of intimacy, but also of being on display (because Four and a group of community leaders are watching her on a big-screen TV). This is where the audience, myself included, erupts in laughter. Moments later, however, Tris needs to knee Four to take control. Kneeing someone also gets a laugh. I swore to myself, because I knew I would have to address this scene later on. My daughter may be tired of all these serious, feminist mom talks, but she has no idea how tired I am from having to start them. Later, we had to talk about how pressuring someone to have sex is never funny.

Making the case for bodily autonomy is difficult under any circumstance—and in particular ways if you are Latina. As a Latino family, we have a culture of piercing our daughter's ears as young as possible. I did not. I chose, instead, to keep her ears intact so she can make that decision herself. It confounded many people when she was an infant. Ear piercing? How could she be upset at that? Why would you want her to consent to it? "Because I want to raise her," I'd reply, "so that consent is *ingrained* in her being." No one touches her body without consent. Sure, we are not at the point where we ask permission for hugs, but I have told her since she was born that her body is hers. Not mine. Not her father's. No one else's.

This body autonomy has reared its head in funny ways. When she was younger, she would use it as a way to stop tickle fights. "Mommy, this is *my* body! No more tickling!" Or when I try to joke with her that since her belly button started as the umbilical cord that I grew for her, that her belly button was mine, I would get back, "No, Mommy. My body. My belly button."

You might be asking yourself if these lectures and this consistent practice of voicing control over her own body pay off. The answer is an adamant yes. The first year she had dance lessons, a boy touched her rear end in class. She immediately stopped him, stopped the class, and reported it to their teacher—who reported it and her clearheaded response to me. Her teacher was both pleased and surprised she had these boundaries and was mature enough to convey a boundary with a peer. Her teacher thanked us for teaching her all of that. I have to admit, her dad and I were so proud. And yes, we told her so.

Maybe all these talks about body autonomy will keep her from letting boys lay their hands on her rear end in the hallway, as if to signal to other boys, "This is mine." I hope this means she knows she can hold hands, perhaps an arm around the waist, but keep ownership signals out of the picture. Okay, yes, holding hands can be seen as ownership, but there is a big difference between two hands clutched together equally and when a boy holds his girlfriend with an arm around her neck, as if preparing to wrestle her to the ground. These are the dotted lines I am attempting to prepare my daughter for once she starts to live a romantic life.

This is the line I walk with my daughter. I want to be open with her about life, not as a friend, but a mom who is not going to simply say, "Wait to have sex until you get married," to avoid a talk about sexuality. And I won't deny that sex and our bodies make us feel good and that we have drives. I have seen my friend, Jaclyn Friedman, say many times that one major flaw in sex education, no matter how progressive, is that we fail to talk about sex as pleasure.

The sexuality of our young people, especially teens, is a national fright. Not so much fear of what they do, but what adults fear them doing. And our leaders are unwilling to face this reality. We can see it in how the country handled the Bill and Monica episode in the late 1990s. President Clinton's insistence that oral sex was not "sexual relations" trickled down to teenagers who reported not having sex (just because it was anal or oral) using the same loophole that the president *leaped* through. When George W. Bush's administration added millions of dollars to abstinence-only sex education, a generation of children grew up being told a list of falsehoods: sex was dangerous, unhealthy, and immoral.

Hitting closer to home for me (and my family), by the end of George W.'s administration, the derogatory term "anchor baby" was used synonymously with "Mexican or Latino undocumented immigrant." It was thrust on women of my heritage because it was believed that pregnant women immigrate to the United States in order to have their children become US citizens by birth. Thus the whole family would benefit from the goodies that being a citizen entails. Never mind that in California a whole industry has popped up that does almost the exact same thing, but with Asian immigrants on "vacation," who happen to give birth in the United States. "Anchor babies" are Mexican.

So what is a parent to do when media—TV, movies, magazine covers—scream out "SEX!" and our society (including the president) is at a loss as to how to express this sexuality in a healthy manner? What do you do when you are a Latina mom, raising a young Latina, knowing that we are part of the demographic that has the highest teen pregnancy rate? When our sexuality is not only stereotyped as willing, but also linked to national immigration policy? What does it mean to symbolize promiscuity itself?

From J. Lo's butt to Sofía Vergara's *cuchi-cuchi* ditzy act, everything about the cultural perception of Latinas screams sex(y). Quick! Picture Salma Hayek! Do you picture the intelligent woman director in glasses sitting behind a camera (one that I have pinned to my office wall) or do you picture the sultry actress with the enviable cleavage? If sex sells, it is deviously lucrative for Latinas.

My daughter will have to navigate this trope once she begins dating. That is one reason why I am so frustrated with the stereotype that Latinas are easy sexual partners. The stereotype primes others as to what a Latina is willing to do sexually. If our bodies are already sexual, is there any way that she can dress modestly and be respected?

So, back to my lectures: after the theft of Jennifer Lawrence's nude photos, I knew we needed a big conversation. My daughter, newly a phone owner, knows that taking appropriate photos is part of her phone contract and I wanted to reinforce this rule. But since a lot of the media around the hacking and

SLUT ON THE LATINA BODY

theft was very shaming of Lawrence and the other women whose photos were stolen, I wanted to clarify that while the taking of nude photos is *not* appropriate for kids, adults can choose whether or not they want to.

I once heard a veteran mom say the best time for awkward or heavy talks is when you are driving. This way you cannot stare at your child, which gives them space to respond. I took a big gulp and waited until I was driving on a stretch of road without streetlights. I started by referencing her contract. She yup'd and uh-huh'd through my review of what she can and cannot do on her phone. I gulped again and explained that over the weekend someone hacked the phones of a lot of actresses and female singers and posted their private photos on the Internet. I explained that nude photos are not appropriate for children to take of themselves, but also said, "Once you are old enough, an adult, you can freely make those sort of decisions." Then I launched into the slut-shaming aspect of the story: "Some people want Jennifer and the other young women to feel bad about taking the photos but—" before I could finish, my daughter responded, "That's not right. It is their business." Win. It was a win because she wasn't even considering that Jennifer was in the wrong or "should have known better." They were adults and could make those decisions. It was wrong to shame them and violate their privacy.

I feel proud of my daughter and myself for how much inner strength she has. The job of raising a girl, especially a Latina girl, with a strong, positive, and protective sense of her body is difficult in our society. Our media tells girls to be sexy, to wear tight clothes, but also that being sexual is bad. As singer Kacey Musgraves says in her song, "Follow Your Arrow," "If you save yourself for marriage, you're a bore / If you don't save yourself for marriage, You're a whore . . . ible person." The virgin-whore conflict is alive and well and in our daughters' lives. On bad days, I wonder how my girl can possibly live in this culture and remain healthy. On good days, I remember that she is already doing it.

When Cyberbullies Attack, Teen Girls Will Fight Back
A Countermeme

JAMIA WILSON

The sweat stains under my armpits betrayed me when my English teacher asked why I was routinely wearing bulky sweaters in one hundred degree Saudi Arabian heat. Perhaps it was the fact that I didn't make eye contact, or maybe it was because I wore the same outfit during lunchtime outside. Or, perchance she heard the tittering of some of my classmates in the schoolyard.

I'll never know how she knew, but Ms. K's sad nod of recognition revealed that she didn't buy my story about the air conditioning being too intense in the classroom. At twelve years old, I was ashamed to reveal that I covered myself in layers to avoid taunts from boys (and some girls seeking validation from them) in my new junior high school. A few months into my middle school experience, I stressed about how to avoid classmates' commentary about my rapidly increasing bust size. The remarks in both English and Arabic came in the form of backhanded compliments from other tween girls, snapped bra straps from boys in pre-algebra class, and rumors being spread about how my "dressing like a slut" and "showing off my boobs" meant I was promiscuous.

As an expat kid growing up in a country where religious and legislative policies literally dictated how much women covered their bodies, the shaming and policing I experienced as my own body morphed into its more voluptuous state impacted my self-image more than anything else. Years later, I experienced similar harrying treatment at an all-girls school started by (of all things) Victorian "Blue-stocking" feminists. The progressive history and sisterhood-driven ethos of our alma mater didn't stop a Twiggy-shaped sophomore from spreading a tale about me being asked to junior prom by her crush at Georgetown Prep. I was outraged when mutual friends informed me that she announced at study hall that he asked me out because I had "slutty ginormous boobs and will probably have sex with him."

Almost fifteen years later, one of the people who gossiped about me attempted to add me on Facebook. I'm usually the forgiving type, but the hurt feelings reemerged and reminded me how much it burned in the first place. As I denied the friend request, I thought, "thank goodness social media didn't exist when this happened to me." My stomach clenched soon thereafter, as I realized that girls and young women are being slut shamed, harassed, and bullied both online and offline, and the trauma and humiliation that often results has led to everything from substance abuse to eating disorders and suicide.

Even though I had a robust network of friends

and caring parents, I was too mortified to share with them my embarrassment and anger about being branded a slut because of how I looked. I suffered in silence and attended to my wounds in private while pretending to brush it off at school. Today's teen targets of cyberbullying are ritualistically confronting similar shaming and stigmatization of their bodies and sexuality in the rapid-fire, unrelenting frontier of the Internet.

Bullying and slut shaming are not new, and neither are the tired and reductive tactics authority figures often suggest to put a Band-Aid on the problem rather than attack its root causes. We often hear old-school adages like "sticks and stones may break your bones, but words will never hurt you," and "ignore bullies at school and turn off your phone and social media if you want to be left alone."

Trite justifications continue to be made that place blame on victims of harassment rather than the deeply seeded conditioning and messaging we've received that stigmatize and malign young women for simply being who they are in patriarchal culture. To be clear, my acknowledgment of how the digital and mobile media landscape complicates and impacts how girls are "slutted" and defamed in schools is not an endorsement for limiting and policing teens' access to technology. This form of cyberbullying stems from the prevalence and normalization of sexism and misogyny in our public institutions and pop culture, and is heightened because of the hyperpublic nature of the digital space. Cyberbullying surfaces the problem in voyeuristic real time for a multitude of eyes to see.

Rape culture is real and intensely hammers itself into our consciousness in a 24-7 media cycle. It's also true that girls are bombarded with an unprecedented amount of sexualized media messaging, and media-perpetuated victim blaming in the aftermath of highly publicized sexual assaults from Maryville to Steubenville. The real problem is our cultural narrative about girlhood, and not the medium itself. Indeed, the same medium that is deployed as a tool for online harassment is also the channel that allows girls (and those who support them) to organize, amplify their voices, document their experiences, and speak truth to power collectively.

Due to the proliferation of technology, young women are more equipped to report their perpetrators (sometimes with video and screenshots as evidence), quickly research legal and community resources, help shape public conversation on their blogs or Tumblrs, and hold complicit policymakers and administrators accountable with wide-reaching digital megaphones in the form of online petitions and memes.

What's more, girls are poised to seek immediate support from their privately curated networks with messaging applications like Snapchat and WhatsApp, and to seek timely confidential guidance from youth-friendly experts via Crisis Text Line, a mobile counseling service for teens in crisis.

Using the power of technology to help, instead of hurt, is integral to transforming our culture. It's challenging for girls to grow and thrive in the midst of a media and social climate that freely perpetuates speculation about the sex lives of stars like Rihanna,

Taylor Swift, and Miley Cyrus because of their attire and their performance styles.

I've witnessed firsthand how girls empower each other when they share their stories in safer online spaces that are judgment-free, youth friendly, and honest, like teen-run *Rookie*, and the girl-fueled SPARK Movement blog. Affirming and supportive online communities like these allow girls to reclaim online space, connect with sympathetic allies, validate their experiences, and discuss them on their own terms.

As a staff writer for *Rookie*, I often receive emails from girls (and sometimes the adults in their lives) sharing that reading personal essays and honest stories about sex, race, gender, and more helps them cope. Most of the girls I've encountered through *Rookie* love the honest thoughtful writing, but equally enjoy connecting with like minds via *Rookie*-related events and the online forum. The most common sentence I've seen in my inbox and in the comments section is, "Thank you. Now I know I am not alone."

What inspires me about girls repurposing tech to drive conversation and create solutions is that they're switching the narrative from one of blame to one of transcendence. That's why I'm inspired by youth who are taking a stand as creators of solutions and movement leaders in a culture that often targets young women as a demographic to vilify for our societal ills.

The increasing accessibility of digital space has enabled girls to move from targets and markets, to makers and creators of media. My heroes include young women like Trisha Prabhu, a fourteen-year-old Google Science Fair finalist whose app works to reduce online harassment between teenagers, Jada, a Houston teen who shared her story on TV when photos of her rape were turned into a nefarious meme, and Erin McKelle, a college student whose column on *The Huffington Post* discusses how her activism saved her life after she survived sexual assault and bullying. Trisha, Jada, and Erin are just a few of the young women who are utilizing the very tools that are being used to undermine, shame, and silence them. They have confronted the problem by creating sites of authentic truth telling, learning, and healing defined by youth for youth.

Their courage is contagious, and I remain in awe of the solidarity girls demonstrate online when others speak up and need support in the face of attacks. The borderlessness of the digital arena allows for girls to come together quickly and publicly, and that in itself is a statement in a culture that perpetuates stereotypes about "mean girls" and their so-called inherent competition. For example, when Jada responded to the mocking #jadapose meme exploiting pictures of her rape by sharing her photo on Instagram with the hashtag #IamJada, she reclaimed her image and in turn, girls and young women from around the world used her hashtag to express their support and share their own stories and solidarity selfies.

In addition to enlivening a movement among young women and girls online, the widespread coverage of Jada's countermeme on outlets like MSNBC and Al Jazeera amplified an important message—

when cyberbullies attack, girls and young women online will fight back.

When I was younger, I didn't have a name for what I experienced, or even understand that it was a prevalent experience countless other young women were enduring. When I discovered Leora Tanenbaum's book *Slut! Growing Up Female With A Bad Reputation* in college, my friends and I passed it around until its paperback covers fell off. I wish I had found it about a decade earlier.

I can't help but wonder what it would have been like if I could have digitally accessed a plethora of other girls' stories, learned about the real reasons behind "slutting" and stereotyping by downloading *SLUT* to my Kindle, and spoken out by writing a blog post about my experience. Today, I'm all about countering cyber hate with a conspiracy of online love, and I'm taking my cues from badass teen girls who are fighting back. While times are more complex for girls growing up online, I'm confident that they will continue to innovate and wield technology productively to communicate, educate, protest, and most importantly, build community with each other.

Dress Codes or How Schools Skirt Around Sexism and Homophobia

SORAYA CHEMALY

Dress codes are the entry point for most adolescent girls to understand sexism.

Spring is coming, which means we are entering the season of the regulation of how much skin girls around the country are allowed to bare. Dress codes, while usually regulating boys' slovenliness, tend to police girls for how much of their bodies are visible. While everyone is in theory affected by dress codes, girls and LGTBQ youth are disproportionately affected by them. Challenging schools to align unexamined, traditional dress codes to contemporary values is a tangible place to start if you're interested in teaching kids to live in a diverse, tolerant society. Of course, many parents are not interested.

When it comes to girls, skimpy and skin-baring clothes are often the primary issue. Kids know that many words, like "unladylike," are code for "slutty." Other words that are frequently used include "distracting" and "unprofessional." Many teachers worry

This piece was adapted from a piece originally published in *The Huffington Post*.

that girls' skin will "so addle boys' brains that they will be unable to concentrate."[1] Boys (and apparently in Iowa, adult men who can now legally fire "irresistible" women), we are told, simply cannot concentrate in this environment.

So, what exactly is wrong with saying girls are "distracting"? I mean, everyone knows this, right?

Who gets to be distracted? And whose distraction is central? What is a girl supposed to think in the morning when she wakes up and tries to decide what to wear to school? They aren't idiots. The logical conclusion of the "distracting" issue is, "Will I turn someone on if I wear this?" Now who is doing the sexualizing? My daughters would never have thought these things without the help of their school. The only people these policies worry about distracting are heterosexual boys. When I was a teenager, there was a boy who distracted the hell out of me. It was the way his hair brushed against his neck and an insouciant ease with his large body. I managed just fine academically, and so can straight boys who encounter girls they are attracted to. When have you ever heard someone talk about what is distracting to girls or gay kids? This idea ignores that fact that girls and LGBTQ kids exist as sexual people. But, do you know what is distracting? Trying not to be distracting. This framing of the problem is marginalizing, sexist, and heteronormative.

1. Jessica Lahey, "A Dress-Code Enforcer's Struggle for the Soul of the Middle-School Girl," *The Atlantic*, February 14, 2013, 1. http://www.theatlantic.com/sexes/archive/2013/02/a-dress-code-enforcers-struggle-for-the-soul-of-the-middle-school-girl/273155/.

In addition, it implies strongly that girls have responsibility for boys' responses and that boys cannot control themselves. Boys should be insulted. People need to get a super-firm grip on the fact that girls are not sexual thermostats for their male peers. Boys need to manage themselves and are fully capable of doing so.

If people are concerned that girls consider themselves decorative or that they think that appearing in what can be construed as sexually provocative ways is important, then they should confront the reasons why girls perceive these things to be true by the time they are ten or eleven. The clothes that our culture makes available and fashionable for girls—the ones tied to being attractive, to glamour, success, money, and public female power and glory—are the same ones that make it possible for most girls and women to access power and resources vicariously in male-dominated culture. *That* is what schools should be concerned with. Blaming girls for making rational choices about what society rewards them for is useless and hypocritical.

This isn't to say girls should go to school wearing anything that strikes their fancy, no matter how skimpy. When their underwear is showing it's not because they're channeling Jean Paul Gaultier in an attempt to show how artificial the construction of gender is. There are times when girls reach an age when being sexy or sexual is just fine, but, in the same way that they shouldn't wear athletic clothes to go to a wedding, they shouldn't wear clothes they'd wear, say, to a concert, when they go to school. I want my girls to be comfortable at school and respectful of their teachers and the learning environment. Boys, too. If this means, as girls occasionally suggest to teachers, that a school talk to boys about not looking at girls' legs if it makes them uncomfortable, then so be it. With uniforms, it should be even simpler. The issue isn't having rules or standards, it's the assumptions with which they are constructed and how they are enforced. This is of much more concern and frequently sets harmful precedents.

Some administrators start every school day with rigorous visual inspections as kids tumble onto campuses. These inspections don't exist in a vacuum. No one is suggesting that teachers are like street harassers but inspections begin around the same time that young girls start experiencing daily street harassment and sexual harassment on campus. In school, boys, like girls, are targets of public humiliation but, especially if they are straight, this type of public inspection and commentary on their bodies and clothes is usually limited to school. For girls and many LGBTQ people, this is just the beginning and it never ends. They have to deal with related feelings amplified by administrators who feel strongly about enforcement. On the recent afternoon of the day that my girls' school reviewed uniform policies, a gaggle of thirteen-year-old girls (in regulation uniforms) piled into my car as two men on the street leered, mumbled "compliments" at them, and laughed. I didn't mention it, but realized the girls heard them as they started talking about how "creepy" it was. One made an automatic and unselfconscious connection: She said she did not like being inspected in school and these unsolicited appraisals felt the same way to her.

It's hard to know, in this context, who a girl is talking about when she says she's "uncomfortable when he winks" at me. I know it seems ridiculous to compare thoughtful, often loving teachers—regardless of gender—with random jerks on the street, but that is true only if you willfully deny the centrality of the thirteen-year-old girls' point of view in the matter of her own comportment. The well-documented harmful effects of self-objectification that result from the policing of school dress regulations is not unlike those that result from street harassment. From the girls' perspective, they'd started their day with people reviewing, having conversations about, and publicly commenting on their bodies and were ending it in the same manner. It's wearisome. Some might say distracting.

In addition, the way school rules are often demonstrated is problematic. For example, administrators might take a girl up to a stage and draw a line on her leg, to show where a regulation-length skirt should fall. This is often done with humor, to offset the unpleasantness and difficulty of the task at hand, and everyone has a good laugh. A girl with no power, being told by a bigger person with authority what to do, might be acquiescing to what is happening to her, but she is not consenting. By using her body as a prop, the enforcer uses her body as an object for his or her purposes. Making it a joke can be insidious. I know this is not what's going through a teacher's head when surrounded by pubescent students who are violating code. But, nonetheless, this happens every day, year after year in some places, and it is a terrible precedent to set for boys and girls.

Our ideas about consent and the use of other people's bodies are important and cannot, in this culture, begin early enough. Take, for example, the fact that 28 percent of girls in college are sexually assaulted (and 3 percent of boys), but only 5 percent report these crimes. Say a boy or group of boys rapes a girl. They have grown up with ideas about how her clothes can "distract" boys and make them do things they haven't been told or asked overtly to control. The girl also might very well have internalized ideas repeatedly conveyed to her about how people confuse her clothes for "morality," or intent, how others can use or comment on her body, how her consent is neither expected nor respected. Not only has she internalized these ideas, but her school might have institutionalized them in dress code policy and enforcement. This is not helpful. According to the Center for Public Integrity, the reason only 5 percent of sexual assault victims report their assault is either because they don't understand the nature of these crimes or because they are only too aware of institutional tolerance for these practices.

Girls' "right to bare arms" is an idea with a long and meaningful tail. This topic must be one of the most difficult for school administrators, often caught between a rock and a hard place with students, parents, their personal beliefs, traditions, and concerns about student safety and performance. There are many ways to consider the usefulness, purpose, intent, and effects of dress codes. If school communities are genuinely worried about girls and boys then they need to examine the stereotypes that permeate their own policies—policies that are sometimes simply palimpsests of sexism, racism, and homophobia, written over time and left undisturbed for too long. When traditions are sexist and homophobic they should be abandoned. What to put in their place? Glad you asked: programs that deal with root issues like cultural gender stereotypes, sexism, and misogyny in media, like the film *Miss Representation* or Common Sense Media's Gender ToolKit or *SLUT*, are good places to start.

Decoding Title IX

SARAH RANKIN

L ike you, at dinner parties, I'm often asked what I
do. I reply, "I'm the Title IX Investigator for MIT."
And then I wait to see what they'll say. Typically, it
goes something like this. "MIT? Ha, they don't have
any sports teams do they?" Polite chuckle. "Yes, they
actually have a very robust athletic department. I
know, football players aren't what you picture when
you think of an MIT student," I say with another
polite chuckle. I may even insert some witty comment about Howard Wolowitz from *The Big Bang
Theory*, depending on my audience. "But my job is
to investigate cases of sexual harassment and relationship violence, which are also considered a form
of gender-based discrimination."

This often ends the discussion—but, if I'm lucky,
may also lead to an interesting conversation about
sexual assault on college campuses, which has
remained rampant for several decades. Around 25
percent of the time, this exchange will lead to the
person disclosing that he or she was assaulted in
college. Or their roommate was, or their sister, or
their daughter. Each person has a different story but

the common theme is that their school never talked about "those things." Usually, they don't remember being told anything at orientation about sexual violence, almost none knew if their school had a policy prohibiting these behaviors, knew that they could report it, or that they had any rights protected under Title IX.

Of late, the media has been focusing a lot on Title IX, but most people have only a vague understanding of it. Title IX, a portion of the Education Amendments of 1972, states: "No person in the United States shall, on the basis of sex, be excluded from participation in, be denied the benefits of, or be subjected to discrimination under any education program or activity receiving federal financial assistance."

When it passed, it was largely applied to athletics, because the National Collegiate Athletic Association was the first entity to challenge the law, hoping to protect college football from the encroachments of equal rights. Title IX advances emerged such as equitable funding for male and female teams, facilities, and coaching staff. In recent years, colleges have been reminded by the Office of Civil Rights (OCR) through a Dear Colleague Letter (DCL) in April 2011 that Title IX also applies to cases of sexual harassment and sexual violence.

What does this mean? Witness this story from the not-so-distant past, before these changes in 2011: I talked to a student about how another student at her school had sexually assaulted her after an on-campus party. She reported him to the school. They held a hearing and found him responsible for sexual misconduct and suspended him for two terms. At that time, the school refused to tell the complaintant the outcome of the hearing, claiming that it was protected information in the respondent's student records. All she knew was that he wasn't around anymore so she assumed he'd been expelled. Fast-forward one year: she was walking to class and rounded a corner, literally running into him. As you might imagine, this shook her up. She wasn't able to attend class, concentrate, or even eat. After contacting her school administration to ask why he was back on campus, she was told once again that this was privileged information that they couldn't share with her. Her need to have enough information to stay safe emotionally, psychologically, physically, and academically was trumped by the rights of the other student, despite the fact that he had been found responsible.

Those kinds of stories were not uncommon before the Dear Colleague Letter. While we are still hearing from students who are experiencing this type of response, colleges are now on notice that they have a legal obligation to provide support, resources, and recourse to the people who say they've been raped, not just the people who have been accused. More than seventy schools are currently under investigation for lack of compliance with Title IX. At best, the Title IX surge means that some schools will become positive places for victims to seek justice and resources. At worst, the new flurry of regulations will become just another compliance issue, where colleges do what they have to to avoid getting in trouble with the Department of Education, but don't fundamentally change campus culture.

From my perspective, one of the most powerful aspects of Title IX is that it has leveled the playing field. Many schools are now focusing on equity throughout the process. They are paying attention to both students' rights and are better understanding what it truly means to see these cases through a civil rights lens. With that in mind, I have compiled a list of ten things you should know about your rights:

- Title IX is a federal civil right that protects students from sex and gender discrimination. It applies to any school, K-12 or higher education, receiving federal funds (which is almost all schools, even private ones).
- A Title IX Coordinator is required at all schools. This person ensures compliance with federal regulations. Students should be able to easily identify who their Title IX Coordinator is, how to contact them, and why they would go to that person.
- When a school knows of an alleged incident of gender-based violence (such as sexual harassment, assault, or rape), they are "on notice" and need to investigate (to the extent possible based on the reporting student's request). Most campuses designate any employee who does not have confidential privilege (such as mental health professionals, rape crisis counselors, clergy, and medical professionals) as "responsible employees" or Title IX reporters. This means they are required to tell their school's Title IX Coordinator when

they become aware of an incident or allegation (even if the student asks them not to tell anyone).

- Given the requirements for mandated reporting, schools should make it clear to students who one can talk to confidentially and who is a Title IX reporter.

- I've been working in higher education since 1999 and have seen hundreds of students being revictimized after an assault when trying to seek justice through their school process. Title IX and the Campus SaVE Act have mandated that schools develop equitable, transparent, and nonbiased methods of investigation and adjudication to address this issue.

- The Office of Civil Rights wants to see schools taking steps above and beyond the bare minimum. For example, a campus climate assessment using surveys or focus groups to identify areas of concern could be used to help your school develop a strategic plan to proactively address these concerns. Have a problem with underreporting? Ask your fellow students what the barriers are to coming forward and work to fix them.

- Your campus should be tracking patterns. One piece of this is paying attention to repeat offenders. Research has shown that the majority of sexual assault perpetrators are repeat offenders. This is one of the many reasons information needs to be collected by a centralized Title IX Coordinator. But there are other patterns we should be paying attention to as well. Tell your Title IX Coordinator what's happening, where the unsafe spaces are, which groups are hosting the "sketchy" parties, and what academic environments are condoning sexual harassment.

- Find your allies. If you have Title IX questions or concerns, find people on your campus (sympathetic faculty, women's centers, LGBTQ centers, diversity offices, etc.) who can help you strategize your approach and think through how you engage those with power.
- Get involved. Sexual assault is a public health issue. It needs to be owned by everybody—students, administrators, faculty, parents, the federal government, local law enforcement, etc. Not one group is going to end it alone.
- Know your rights. An informed student can be a powerful advocate for change. A great resource is the Know Your IX website: KnowYourIX.org.

The Global Slutting of Female Sexuality

An Interview with Yasmeen Hassan

THE ARTS EFFECT ALL-GIRL THEATER COMPANY

The Arts Effect recently had the privilege of interviewing Yasmeen Hassan, the Global Director of the human rights organization Equality Now. We discussed the impact of sexism, shaming, and gender-based violence on women and girls around the world.

THE ARTS EFFECT: *What is Equality Now? What does your organization do to support girls and women who are subjected to sexual violence or gender-based violence and injustice?*

YASMEEN HASSAN: Equality Now is the first international human rights organization formed specifically to ensure that the rights of women and girls are included in mainstream human rights discourse. At the time we were formed, women's rights were not seen as international human rights; they were seen as matters of domestic concern. So, it was left to the national governments to do what they will. We were formed to elevate girls and women's rights to an international level by making people see that what happens to women and girls around the world is no less pervasive, severe, or damaging than what happens to political prisoners or what may happen to men in war. We have made significant progress toward our goals in the last twenty-two years.

Our program areas are: discrimination in law, sexual violence, sex trafficking, and female genital mutilation. Laws have been enacted all over the world addressing these issues and more than half the sex discriminatory laws we have campaigned against have been amended or revoked. We work with grassroots groups on the ground in almost every country in the world, and have offices in London, Nairobi, New York, a presence in Jordan, where we do all our Middle Eastern work, and a presence in Washington, DC. We connect policy-level work at the United Nations, at the State Department, at the European Union, and at the African Union to grassroots activists on the ground.

TAE: *Does slut shaming exist in other countries? How is it similar and different to what we see here in the United States?*

YH: What you call slut shaming is an example of exerting power or control on a woman's sexuality. So what appears to be slut shaming in Europe, America, or in Canada is the same thing that we see in places like Afghanistan or Saudi Arabia, where women are completely covered and segregated. We had cases of "morality police" patrolling these countries to enforce the dress codes—women were hit if their ankles were showing or if a strand of hair escaped the hijab. So it's all about denying a woman control over her body to reinforce the control of men. It is part of the patriarchal game plan. Female genital mutilation (FGM), child marriage, and so-called "honor" crimes are all manifestations of the same issue—appropriating a girl's sexuality. You cut off the clitoris, you sew up the vagina to enforce chastity and the control of men. You marry a girl off as a child to exert control over her and her sexuality and reproduction. You enforce such norms of girls through the threat of violence—often mislabeled as an honor killing—where a girl is killed for any perceived indiscretion with a man who is not her husband. We see this all over the world. We see it in many countries of Africa, the Middle East, and Latin America where girls are forced to marry their rapists to salvage their honor. While manifestations of power are different in different places, the end result is the same—controlling a girls' sexuality and appropriating her reproduction.

TAE: *Just as we're experiencing an epidemic of rape on high school and college campuses here in the United States, India and the Democratic Republic of Congo are facing homegrown rape crises. What are the common factors? What are the differing factors?*
YH: The biggest common factor is the lower status given to women and girls. In the United States, people think we have reached equality. When I grew up it was very clear there were certain inequalities and we knew things were not equal. Many young women who are growing up these days believe the age of feminism was the sixties and seventies. We watch these inequalities play out in various scenarios such as rape on campus. Boys' sexuality is regarded as

"Oh, he's so cool—he's such a dude" and girls are "sluts." That is not equal. Often young girls in this country don't realize that there is a problem until they hit the workforce. When they are very young and still in school there is a dream that we are in an equal world—even our sexual rights are equal—then they get a shock when something goes wrong and they are not believed or supported.

But in places like India, there is no pretense that women and men are equal. Look at the sex ratio. There is sex-selective abortion; people grieve when women give birth to girls. In a documentary on women in India sponsored by Gucci, a Miss India winner told the story of how her mother left her father when she was born as the father and her family wanted her smothered to death because she was the second girl. That story illustrates the perceived the value of girls—zero. When you look at the statistics in that country, the demographics, girls are shorter than boys, they get much less food and education than boys, and they are seen as an economic burden. There is a dowry that the father has to give to marry off his daughter and take her off his hands. This lower value of girls plays out across society and results in devastating violations.

When you talk about the Democratic Republic of Congo you can see that wherever there is conflict or economic recession, the first thing to be attacked is the status and the rights of women, and violence against women exponentially increases. The fact that so many women were raped in the war is because women were seen as the honor and the property of their families and not as individuals. They were raped to destroy the community. Those women were then shunned by their community. Why would a family be destroyed if a member is raped? It's because you are the property of your family. So all of it is about inequality.

TAE: *How is rape glorified in different cultures around the world? And why?*

YH: We talked about wars, economic recession, and the devaluing of women. Another important factor to consider is the role of popular culture in reinforcing dangerous stereotypes that glorify rape—all done in the name of entertainment! Several years ago we campaigned against a Japanese game called Rape-Lay. In the game you are a penis—literally a penis—and you stalk young girls, prepubescent girls, and their teenage sisters and their mothers in subways. You then rape them, torture them, and force them to abort any babies they might have. That's how you score points. Also, the more blood you splatter in the rape the better because that means you got a virgin. This was actually a game that was available on Amazon and sold throughout Japan. We got it taken off Amazon, and we got the gaming industry in Japan to self-regulate. But, the point is, there is a culture in Japan (and many other places, I'm just using Japan as an example) that supports this type of entertainment. There was a popular comic there too called *Rape Man*. The main character is a guy who is a teacher by day and at night he rapes his students. So they have fetishized schoolgirls.

When we took on this issue, we got a lot of backlash. We were sent a video of what appeared to be a girl being raped in Japan in a train. We sent it to Japanese police and their response was that this was not a minor because "we can see from the pubic hair that she is older" and they would not investigate. We received hate mail from all over the world and rape and death threats. We have never had as strong a reaction to any campaign we have done and we've taken on honor crimes, female genital mutilation, acid throwing, and stove burning—but pornography? Seems like many men are very attached to their right to entertain themselves with violence against women.

The same subjugation of women can be seen in the advertisements you see here in New York when you're just walking your children to school—younger and younger girls posed in sadomasochistic scenes, or being choked, or lying there like dead bodies with male models posed over them to sell luxury brands and, along the way, glamorize and reinforce the subjugation of women.

TAE: *Help us connect the dots. How is the "slutting" of female sexuality tied to other challenges girls and women face worldwide? For example: Sextrafficking? FGM? Child Marriage?*
YH: Perceptions of the role of women and girls help shape the culture and the violations that will be culturally tolerated and condoned. Equality Now works to ensure that legal systems around the world work to prevent violations of women's and girls' rights. When you have a culture where women are blamed for their abuse—whether there is a "slutting" culture or a culture where a woman's body represents the

honor of her family—it is very hard to make the legal system work. The people who are part of that system—police, prosecutors, judges, parliamentarians—are also a part of that culture.

I'll give you an example. In Pakistan we did a study of all cases that dealt with incest. There is no law against incest in Pakistan. We went through twenty years of cases and if an incest case by chance even made it to court—which mostly they don't because there's so much stigma and shame and victim blaming—the judges dismissed the case, based in part on blaming and doubting the victim. The only favorable judgment for an incest survivor was in the case of a five-year-old girl who was raped by her brother and the mother walked in on the rape.

Various harmful traditional practices and sex stereotyping of women also shape men's sexual pleasure. For example, FGM is a way of controlling female sexuality so that women's and girls' sexual pleasure is taken away and instead they experience pain while the man's sexual pleasure may become tied to the discomfort of the woman. In some countries where FGM is practiced, I've heard that many men can now only get aroused by a woman who is mutilated and that the longer it takes to penetrate her and the more pain there is the better. After childbirth, women are stitched up again and doctors will look to the man and say, "How tight?"

Similarly, the porn culture in this country has also resulted in men being aroused by "porn sex" where sex is completely divorced from love and emotions.

The common denominator is that women are

blamed everywhere. I come from a Muslim country. I was taught from the time I was thirteen years old to keep myself covered—to not wear transparent clothes or sleeveless clothes so as not to excite men. Any transgression that results in your being harassed is your fault. There are no corresponding codes for men and in fact men are viewed as lacking any self-control at all, excusing all forms of violence against women. It is easy to pass this off as cultural mores, but such culture seems to me built on the backs of women. Look at the problems women are having with sexual harassment in Egypt. Such mores are being used to silence women and deny them access to public spaces! We have to realize that what is passed off as culture all over the world serves as a system of male control over women. In my mind, culture is dynamic and ever-evolving, it is positive, it is to be celebrated. It should never be seen as static and serve to entrench a system of inequality.

TAE: *Agreed! But the sexism that perpetuates the abuse of women and girls is sometimes deeply rooted in cultural tradition and religious beliefs. How do we as a global community address this reality?*

YH: Culture is supposed to be dynamic. Culture is when people live together as a collective whole; they define certain norms of what they want to live by. Culture has never remained static, ever. Culture evolves. What is amazing to me is that things that have to do with women and family suddenly become static. This is justified in the name of religion and religious edicts. The oppression of people cannot be a part of culture. You cannot perpetuate oppression in the name of culture or in the name of religion.

When I look at Islamic law, for example, which I studied, it is very clear that over time almost all Muslim countries have been flexible about how Islamic law against interest has been (or rather not been) applied to investments, showing great flexibility in adapting religious edicts to the needs of the time. However, by and large you find great inflexibility in the Islamic laws that are applied to women and the family—systems of male guardianship over women persist, women do not have equal rights of inheritance, women do not have equal rights in marriage and divorce, or rights of custody of their children, polygamy is allowed, etc. Almost every religion has been used to keep women down and the power of interpretation has almost never been given to women in any religion. The interpreters of religion are men and many injustices—FGM, child marriage, lack of reproductive rights, you name it—have been justified on the basis of religion. I feel that unless we are able to change with our new understandings of the world, we will be lost. Currently, culture and religion are mostly used to resist change.

TAE: *In your opinion, what steps need to be taken in order to shift the tide globally?*
YH: To change the tide, I think we have to shift the international perspective. This is actually why Equality Now was formed. What we see is there are always pockets of grassroots groups around the world who

are fighting to solve problems as they see them within their communities. But, these groups are the most marginalized because they are touching very hot button topics for that community. I would consider The Arts Effect to be one of these grassroots groups. You are taking on issues of girls' rights in the United States (and around the world) and these are very difficult topics that make people uncomfortable. People don't want to listen. The same things happen to our activists working on child marriage in Yemen, or female genital mutilation in Kenya. These are hard things to talk about. They are conversations people don't want to have and governments certainly don't want to listen to. We often hear governments say, "Oh, young girls? Why is this a priority? Let's focus on the war with so-and-so or let's work on GDP." Our main goal is to educate the international community so they know about these issues and then come together to solve these issues. And I think we've been quite successful in that most violations have been exposed and are known. I think the first steps are to know about the issues, connect the dots, and make sure that people know this is all in continuum. So we no longer say honor killings are Jordan's problem or FGM is Kenya's problem or rape in Steubenville is the United States' problem—these are manifestations of problems women and girls face around the world. Connecting the issues and connecting women and girls to create a global movement is really vital.

As women, I find we are often divided from each other. Whether it's on the basis of race, class, or nationality, there are so many factors that pull us apart. When we talk about a women's movement or a girls' movement, we need to get buy in across races, nationalities, economic classes, ages, and also gender. One way patriarchy works is by dividing women and girls from each other. In so many slut shaming cases in the United States, girls are often the ones being brutal to each other and pitting themselves against one another over a guy. In places like Pakistan, India, and the Middle East, domestic violence is violence perpetrated by mother-in-law against daughter-in-law, and FGM is carried on by female circumcisers. As feminists, we need to reject that system and have a system of solidarity with other women and girls and reclaim our lives.

TAE: *What are two things we must do to change the world for women and girls?*
YH: First, it is critical that girls and women understand their rights. Every time I hear from survivors they say they didn't speak out because they felt it was their fault, they did something wrong. We have to work with women and girls so they feel empowered to know their rights and work with law enforcement and the justice system to respect those rights.

Second, international action is extremely important. All governments come together at the United Nations. So, when the United Nations sets certain standards, even if they might not filter down, they are going to be listened to much more actively than anything that can be done at the national level. Taking these issues to the international level elevates the issues, protects marginalized groups that may be at risk because now their governments know that the international community is watching, and allows for laws and policies to be put into place. Laws and policies are not the sexiest things for people to work on, I understand that—but they are critically important. Ultimately, if you are a citizen of any part of the world, who should be accountable to you? Your government. You need to get laws and policies in place that treat men and women equally. And when they are not being treated equally, systems have to be set up so that women have access to justice. A well-functioning legal system does not result in many people in jail, but rather people deterred from committing crimes.

Recent research suggests that when men and women are treated more equally, there's less conflict within society. There are fewer wars, less internal conflict, and society functions much better. Very high up on that gender equality index list are a lot of the Nordic countries. According to the World Bank, progress is dependent on equality within the basic unit of society—the home. This is something women's rights activists have known for decades so I am glad the World Bank backed it up! If from the time you are born, you are not equal to your brother, then your choices are very limited. You carry that inequality with you throughout your life. And all sorts of sexual violence and violations happen because you are less than a man.

So, two major things have to happen in order to create change. First, knowledge: women have to know, they have to be made aware, and they have to work together and claim their rights. And men have to be educated on those rights as well. Second, laws: legal systems have to be equipped to deliver those rights. And these things have to be delivered in tandem. I think with these two things, we can change the world. Honestly, I do.

Teaching *SLUT*
Empowering Students to Understand Slut Shaming and Rape Culture

ILEANA JIMÉNEZ

Teaching about gender-based violence is a critical part of the work I do in a high school course I teach on feminism and activism. The most productive way to teach and learn about these topics is to let students lead, starting from narratives that they create based on their own lives that are inspired by the readings, films, and guest speakers that are an integral part of the course. Inspired by these texts, students then uncover their own history and experiences, speak truth to power, and create their own community-specific approaches to changing rape culture.

One early exercise that I have students do in my feminism class—which has attracted both young women and men every time I offer it—is to reflect on their initial associations with feminism, why they are in the course, and what they would like to learn. Because I want my students to be a part of designing my course as much as I am, I use these early reflections as part of my planning process, and even include excerpts of their writing in my course overview. One Puerto Rican girl, Paris, wrote in the fall of 2013:

> Look down the street. Thirteen-year-old girls are being killed for speaking their mind; girls and women alike are being taken and trafficked every day; walk down the street and notice any girl or woman being harassed and catcalled for what they are wearing.

When I read words such as Paris's, I am reminded of the important journey that this course is for them and how, from the very start, we are working in partnership with each other to create change. I came to do this work on slut shaming and rape culture with high school students through the street harassment movement.

But I knew that street harassment wasn't the only form of harassment that my students were facing. I knew that it was also happening at school. A few years ago, I read a book by Brooklyn-based Girls for Gender Equity (GGE), *Hey Shorty! A Guide to Combating Sexual Harassment and Violence in Schools and on the Streets* (published, like *SLUT*, by the Feminist Press). Coauthored by GGE's founder Joanne Smith along with then-GGE staffers Mandy Van Deven and Meghan Huppuch, this slim, powerful volume opened up an entire roadmap for how to address gender-based violence in schools. I'd read the book while doing Fulbright research on queer youth in high schools in Mexico City. One approach that spoke to me from *Hey Shorty!* was their description of partnering with graduate students and academics at the City University of New York (CUNY) to conduct a participatory action research project (PAR) on sexual harassment in school contexts. As part of this PAR project, the girls in GGE's Sisters in Strength group conducted extensive surveys of students on sexual harassment in public schools throughout New York City.

Working alongside CUNY's PAR team, GGE girls led the effort designing questions, collecting data, and evaluating findings. I was inspired by the girl-led focus of the project, especially since GGE works mainly with girls of color from all over New York and their approach has always been a social justice-based feminism with an intersectional framework, which is similar to the one that I use in my classroom. Reading about GGE's project convinced me that PAR projects were one way to engage feminist academia and feminist teachers and their students together in ways that could lead to transformative change in schools.

I also knew that I wanted to learn more about what my students were experiencing at school in terms of sexual harassment and slut shaming and PAR was one way to do that. That's when Deb Tolman, professor of psychology at the Silberman School of Social Work at Hunter College and at the CUNY Graduate Center, and I decided to do a PAR project with the girls at my school. Rather than house the project within my feminism class, though, we decided to open up participation for all students through a class period at my school called X block. X block classes are led by teachers who want to launch a new course in an experimental stage and engage students in the process of designing it with them. Deb and I called our experimental class Sex and the City: Teen Girls and Sexuality.

We met once a week for three months in the fall of 2013. What emerged from this class, which was made up of five sophomore girls who had never taken my feminism class and one senior girl who had, cemented my commitment to discussing slut shaming and rape culture with young people, and opened up new avenues of learning and advocacy for my ongoing feminism class. What was meant to be a short-term project turned into an entire unit in my course.

The girls Deb and I worked with designed an online survey about sex, sexuality, and slut shaming that was sent out to the entire school. Once they collected their findings, the girls made a video highlighting the data and shared it with teachers during a faculty meeting. The most distressing findings included the fact that out of a coed school population of slightly over 200 students, eighty-two responded to the survey, and out of those eighty-two, 62 percent of the girls said they had been called a slut; a striking 72 percent of those girls had called other girls a slut; and 43 percent of those girls had heard the word slut being used at least once a week.

Of the boys who responded, 59 percent had called a girl a slut. In contrast to the 72 percent of girls who had heard a girl being called a slut at least once a week, only 24 percent of the boys reported *ever* hearing the word slut being used against a girl. After reading through these findings, I realized that there was a lot more work to do and I was going to use my feminism class to help transform our school's climate.

Even before the PAR project was launched, the girls in my high school feminism class were writing about slut shaming on our class blog, *F to the Third Power*. One of the things I learned early on in teaching feminism to high school students was that I needed to engage young people in the feminist discourse happening online. For many of my students, whether male or female, feminist blogging launched the articulation of their newly found feminist consciousness. For some of my students, this meant speaking out on their own experience of slut shaming. One Dominican girl, Kaitlyn, wrote a post for the site titled, "I Need Feminism Because of Slut Shaming and Other Double Standards." Kaitlyn wrote this piece as part of the "I need feminism" meme that was popular at the time. In it she reflected:

> I remember hearing the word "slut" for the first time in fourth grade. I was in a group of girls and one boy was gossiping about people in the grade that had graduated the year before. They began to talk about this one girl in particular who happened to be dating a guy that was in my year. As young as we were, this guy had three girlfriends, and was praised for it. But the girl that we were talking about was called a slut. Why? Because she was dating a guy who had three girlfriends, though she didn't know this detail, and was also older than he was.
>
> After that, I became aware that the word "slut" was actually quite ubiquitous. The girls that devel-

oped faster than the rest of us were called sluts. The girls that had their first kisses already were called sluts. If a girl had the nerve to talk about sex, she was called a slut. If a girl's shirt revealed the top of her cleavage she was called a slut. If a girl had sex with more than one guy during her high school career, she was called a slut and "easy."

Blog posts such as these are written as part of our ongoing conversation in class about feminist theory and history, media and activism. During the first month of the course, I spend most of my time providing the theoretical framework that will guide the rest of the course. After each unit, students then blog about their particular interests based on readings they have done. Essentially, these blog posts reveal how they are applying feminist theory to their everyday experiences. These readings include texts by feminists such as bell hooks, the Combahee River Collective, Audre Lorde, Cherríe Moraga, Barbara Smith, Alice and Rebecca Walker, and selections from collections such as *Colonize This! Young Women of Color on Today's Feminism*, as well as a variety of online articles by today's feminist writer-activists such as Jasmine Burnett, the Black Women's Blueprint, and Chimamanda Ngozi Adichie's now famous TED talk "We should all be feminists." These readings and videos provide the intersectional scaffolding that allows students to apply feminist theory not only to themselves and their experiences but also to their communities and the larger world.

Teaching a feminism class in New York provides tremendous opportunities for my students to apply feminist thinking to the larger world. When I took my students to go see *SLUT* during its first run in the fall of 2013, for example, I requested that they use their newly learned intersectional lens while viewing the production. I did not want them to simply watch the production without some kind of guiding framework to help them analyze the storyline and its characters. In addition to a frighteningly realistic depiction of an assault, the play offers specific socioeconomic markers that are familiar to my students, who are a combination of young people who both live in the New York upper middle-class areas mentioned in the script as well as those who live far outside of those neighborhoods. Cool Greenwich Village street names such as Horatio, elite cross streets such as Park and 89th and 78th and Lex, and middle-class enclaves such as Stuyvesant Town, mark our journey with Joey as she tells us her mind-numbing story about being raped by two of her private-school guy friends. In Joey's world, friends make "college lists" with Harvard as a plausible reach school and Wesleyan as a safety. They wear mom's Dolce Vita boots and shop at Urban Outfitters and drink coffee at Starbucks. On the night I saw the play, the cast was made up of seven white girls and four girls of color.

When we spoke of the play later, my students revealed that the world of *SLUT* is both familiar and unfamiliar. Some live in it and some don't, but regardless of their socioeconomic status, like Joey and her friends, all are surviving the same highly competitive school climates where getting into top-name colleges is key. One of the reasons why I bring up socio-economic class and higher education as part of my discussions of the play with my students is that according to some characters, Joey has somehow ruined her guy friend's chances of going to Harvard and getting scouted because she speaks out against their raping her. I want my students to make connections between the worlds they live in and the kind of "boys will be boys" sexist protection high school and college-aged rapists receive when girls and women speak out against their perpetrators.

In addition, for all of my students, regardless of gender and sexual identity, sex and sexuality is a part of school politics. This year, the students in my feminism class are queer, straight, African American, Asian, Bengali, Latino, and white. In the recent past, the course has also attracted transgender students, international students from Australia, Eritrea, Italy, and Palestine, and students whose parents are undocumented. Given the diversity of the students who take my feminism class, my asking them to read the play with an intersectional lens is an assignment that is always met with keen interest.

One white student, Nora, a senior, blogged about how she personally connected with Joey:

> Joey speaks up after being assaulted in the back of a cab on the way to a party. Since Joey is perceived by her school community as a slut, she is not the 'perfect victim' and is therefore not believed or supported by many who learn about her rape.

Personally, I was able to relate to this character, Joey, in how we are both perceived by the world. We are of the same race (white) and similar in socioeconomic status (middle-class). The social situations that Joey is in throughout the play were also candidly depicted and reflected my particular reality as a white, middle-class teenager in New York City. But I know it's not the reality of all teens in New York.

In contrast, another white student, Saskia, a senior, who saw the play during its 2014 limited engagement, analyzed race and class from another angle. She wrote in an in-class reflection:

I thought the play demonstrated the intersection of privileges more than the intersection of oppressions: the majority of the girls were white, lived in affluent sections of Manhattan . . . The play did not go into the experiences of girls of color . . . I think it could have easily been done. Then, however, it would not be such an accurate portrayal of this insular community.

For two students of color in the class who saw the same production as Saskia, the play raised questions about bystander guilt. Diandra, an African American girl, and Emilio, a Latino boy, wanted a way to understand why Tim does not try to stop his friends from raping Joey. Together, they decided to write a monologue for Tim, whose voice we never hear in the play. Even if the monologue itself doesn't explain why he doesn't intervene, for my students, imagining what Tim might've been feeling was a way to begin thinking about the importance of breaking the cycle of violence by reflecting on heteronormative codes of masculinity and sexuality and the ways in which these codes not only restrict but also silence young men and boys from speaking out against rape culture.

Here is what they wrote for Tim:

It was supposed to be a regular night of having fun. Just a little pregaming before a huge party at Connor's. Nothing out of the ordinary. I got to George's house a little early and Luke was already there playing a game of Mario Kart, a bottle of Absolut cracked open. "Well, shit," I thought, "It's lit then!"

After a couple of rounds of Mario Kart, we just waited for Joey to come so we could get going. But then Luke started going crazy saying, "Yo, Joey's so hot. I'd smash." I looked up from my phone in disbelief. I said, "Bro chill, it's Joey." George chimed in with a, "So? She's still crazy hot. And she'd definitely let me hit it first."

Immediately, Luke and George jumped up and got in each other's faces like they were trying to prove they were "badass." They didn't say anything, they just stared. Then George backed down with a glint in his eyes. "Fine," he said, "Let's wait till she gets here."

Still in shock, I looked at the both of them. "Yo, what the fuck, it's Joey!"

Luke kinda lost his temper and turned to me. "Bro, are you gay or something?"

"Chill, you know I'm not gay, but you guys

are really saying fucked up stuff right now. It's Joey. We grew up with her! She's like a sister or something!"

"Speak for yourself," George said while giving Luke a high five, "I guess it will just be me and Luke getting some tonight."

The doorbell rang and we heard Joey's voice from the other side. I could already tell it wasn't going to be one of those regular nights. Later we piled in a cab to go to Connor's and I saw the glint in George's eyes again. I tried to open my mouth to warn Joey, but no sound came out and the music was much too loud. I felt a sinking feeling in my stomach, and I realized that I couldn't move, I couldn't do anything. I just looked out the window and daydreamed. I didn't want it to be real. It couldn't be. I just sat in the cab, hoping that if I acted like nothing was happening, it would be just that.

For the students who wrote this monologue, it was more than just a creative writing exercise. It was an exercise in looking at themselves as young men and women in high school who could very well have found themselves in a similar situation as Joey, George, Luke, and Tim's. A group of boys in the class also wound up performing the scene for our International Day of the Girl assembly, which is led annually by my feminism class. The scene was performed by two African American boys, Jaron and Jayson, along with Emilio, who had cowritten the scene with Diandra. After they performed the scene, Jaron said to the audience: "After seeing Tim be a bystander in *SLUT*, and after speaking to guest activists from Breakthrough who work on behalf of gender-based violence, we learned that most men are not violent, but a lot of men are silent, which is why there is such a need for us to speak up and *be that guy* who stands up for girls and women in the face of violence."

My experience of using *SLUT* as a curricular tool has been and continues to be rewarding, both because the dramatic narrative provides so many entry points for identification and analysis and because the topic of slut shaming and rape is so endemic to the high school experience. For fellow high school English and humanities teachers who are ready to take on a social justice- and feminist-based approach to talking about gender-based violence, *SLUT*'s text invites multiple interpretations, especially given the many conversations it will generate about girls, slut shaming, and sexuality; boys, hypermasculinity, and violence; victim blaming, bystander intervention, and silence. Indeed, its many allusions to popular culture will allow students to feel immediately connected, especially since so many of the texts we teach in our classes are often far removed from the everyday experiences of our students. I have often run out of time in class as students not only share their intersectional analysis of the text but also their personal stories. Students have left both the theater and the classroom wanting to tease out as much of their personal connection to the storyline as their desire to understand why they find the play both problematic for and emblematic of their time.

Given the play's multiple entry points, teachers

may want to take these practical steps before engaging in the text of the play:

- Provide students with an opportunity to reflect on and share their understanding of gender and sexuality, especially in connection to the messages they have received about these categories of identity from family, media, school, and friends. Have them think about these messages in connection to their cultural contexts as well, such as their racial, ethnic, and religious backgrounds. Texts such as Jamaica Kincaid's "Girl" are an excellent starting point, especially since slut shaming is an explicit part of the narrative.
- Build on these conversations by providing students with readings by feminists such as Kimberlé Crenshaw, Angela Davis, bell hooks, Audre Lorde, Cherríe Moraga. Include global perspectives as well, such as Chimamanda Ngozi Adichie's TED talk "We should all be feminists."
- Engage students on their ideas about slut shaming and the varying ways in which the word slut can be interpreted across different communities. Use the essay "Open Letter from Black Women to the SlutWalk" by the Black Women's Blueprint to teach students that not all women embrace the word slut, as demonstrated in this line from the piece: "we do not have the privilege or the space to call ourselves 'slut' without validating the already historically entrenched ideology and recurring messages about what and who the Black woman is."

- Read the play or attend a production of *SLUT*.
- Invite students to write new scenes for the play from their own perspectives.
- Create a class blog, Tumblr, or other social media site to document student responses.
- Engage the larger school in a discussion about school climate in relation to sexual harassment, slut shaming, and rape culture. One entry point of discussion might be to talk about school dress codes, school handbooks that outline codes for behavior, and other school codes of ethics.
- Hold a town hall meeting or an assembly led by informed students and teachers and engage school leaders such as the student council to support the conversation.

We are all accountable for this work in schools. It's not enough to say that the sex educator in the next classroom will take care of this issue. Or the principal. Or the school handbook. Teaching *SLUT* opens not only opportunities for discussion for our students but also opportunities for collective change. If the English teacher covers *SLUT*, and the sex educator covers healthy consent, and the principal and the student council create inclusive guidelines for students that take into account sexual harassment, slut shaming, and rape culture, then we will definitely be on our way to creating a better world not just for Joey, but for George, Luke, and Tim, and indeed, for all of our students.

It's Time to StopSlut
The Rise of the StopSlut Movement

KATIE CAPPIELLO and MEG McINERNEY

D oing something has been the best form of healing for me," said a seventeen-year-old friend of
ours. Chloe is a gifted writer and athlete. She's also
a date-rape survivor, and over the past year she's
turned to activism as a way of processing her experience and fighting back. "It's given me a positive out-
let for my anger, pain, frustration . . . all the things
I've been feeling over the past year. I can't change
what happened to me but being an activist gives me
the power to change things for others."

For survivors, those at risk, everyday citizens,
and young people no matter the gender, speaking
out about the prevalence of sexual shaming and violence in our communities is key to challenging the
status quo, creating a healthier, safer sexual climate,
and empowering those who are often silenced. Laws
are established, changed, and finally enforced, and
cultural attitudes shift, only when we collectively
say enough is enough—every voice matters in this
fight.

And we get it, acting up often feels burdensome
in the midst of midterms, rushing your dream soror-

ity or fraternity, balancing your day job with planning for your dream job, getting your kid through eighth grade, preparing the semester's syllabus . . . but we've seen activism exist effectively in every form. There's a misconception that taking social action has to look and feel a specific way. It doesn't. The only required ingredient in activism is action. Whether just opening your eyes to your own prejudices, or raising awareness about slut shaming and rape on your news feed, or taking it to the streets with bullhorns and picket signs, your efforts will make an impact—and, in the process, make you bold.

Over a recent dinner with Matt, the now twenty-one-year-old college junior whom we both babysat for in our early New York City days, he hit the nail on

---

STOPSLUT EVENT AT LYNN REDGRAVE THEATER IN NEW YORK CITY:
A twenty-year-old man admitted, "This is sort of embarrassing but . . . I want to be real here . . . not sure what I would do if I saw my friends violating a girl. And that scares me. I'm not sure I would know how to intervene. What's the solution to that, you know?"

"Practice?" quipped a thirteen-year-old boy.

A sixteen-year-old girl responded, "Yeah, we all need to practice how to take action as bystanders— whether we call someone out, or just step between a girl being groped and the guy, or find a way to distract the guy. We all need to come up with plans."

The thirteen-year-old boy added, "Yeah and we have to say 'fuck it' and not worry about people calling us pussies or whatever . . . that's the hard part. Because that is not the type of man we should all want to be. I don't want to be that guy."

---

the head: "When people speak out they give others permission to do the same. Personally, I'm in awe of the young guys who have taken action by simply telling the truth—speaking so candidly about the same pressures I felt in middle school, high school, and now still in college. When one person opens up about porn addiction, the sexual double standard, or their regrets as an inactive bystander, discussion happens. We're no longer isolated. It takes balls to act." We move on, eat pizza, talk about music, and the beauty of vinyl, then circle back: "You know, there's this fear that it will be social suicide to talk about rape and slut culture, that people will judge you but that actually happens far less than you'd think—because this shit affects us all."

STOPSLUT EVENT AT THE HAMMER MUSEUM:
A middle school teacher from LA asked, "How do I deal with my young female students who dress provocatively? I don't want to slut shame them, but I'm tired of seeing them disrespect themselves by wearing low-cut shirts and short shorts?"

An eighth grade girl tearfully responded, "Countless days I've gone home from school in tears because a teacher has told me in front of the whole class that I'm dressed inappropriately and distracting everyone . . . it would be so much better if teachers just talked to me one-on-one and, to be honest, why do teachers think that wearing a tank top means I don't respect myself? Why is humiliation the tactic you all use? Teachers claim to want me to respect myself, but they don't show me respect—I don't feel respected when it comes to my body."

The reality is everyone is touched by slut and rape culture, and consciously or not, we're all contributors and victims. So, the question is: How will you be part of the solution?

For us, the answer is creating this play and launching StopSlut, a youth-driven activist movement to end sexual shaming and violence on middle school, high school, and college campuses.

In our over twelve years of teaching, we've seen and heard a strong desire to engage in social justice action from youth across the world. Often, young people just don't know where to start (which is actually true for people of all ages). They sometimes haven't yet realized the power they possess or discovered how to access it. That's where StopSlut comes in: StopSlut uses cultural expression to highlight universally felt social injustices and empower

---

STOPSLUT EVENT AT NORTH DAKOTA STATE UNIVERSITY:

A fifteen-year-old girl stood shaking, holding her friend's hand, trying to catch her breath, "I am going to say this for this first time . . . because being silent is literally making me sick . . . I was raped. And for the longest time, I've felt so alone. And I just want to know, why don't we talk about it?"

"You're not alone," answered a sixteen-year-old girl. "I was raped too. At a party. I was a sophomore."

"I was raped," said a twenty-six-year-old woman. Then a sixty-five-year-old woman remarked, "I was raped. And clearly it's time for this community to open its eyes. Being scared and staying silent because this issue makes us upset or uncomfortable is not working. "

---

young people to create their own responses to slut shaming, rape, and sexism.

The goals of StopSlut are:

- Offer spaces for people of all ages to come together to process common but often silenced experiences.
- Educate communities on slut shaming culture and its connection to rape culture.
- Provide tools (a play script, workshop model, discussion questions, and activism templates) for healthy action including bystander intervention before an assault occurs and victim/survivor support.
- Promote the philosophy of CARE—Communication, Accountability, Respect, and Empathy for all.

In conjunction with the play's premiere in 2013, we launched the StopSlut Movement with the inaugural meeting of the StopSlut Coalition (which you'll learn more about soon!) and a two-day event at the New School in Manhattan—StopSlut: A Conference on Sexuality, Bullying, and Rape. Copresented by The Arts Effect, the Feminist Press, the New School, Equality Now, Soapbox, Inc., and St. Francis College, the conference was attended by over 425 middle, high school, and college students from New York, New Jersey, and Connecticut, all of whom gave up their Friday night and full Saturday to engage in groundbreaking discussions. The conference agenda was composed of expert-led panels on "History of 'Slut'," "The Role of the Bystander," "What can you do?" and real stories of slut shaming and rape from young women and men ages thirteen to eighteen, and a performance of *SLUT*, followed by a Q&A. Guest speakers and panelists included: Michaela Angela Davis, Amy Richards, Jamia Wilson, Emily May, Wagatwe Sara Wanjuki, Lisa Brunner, Christen Clifford, Anastasia Higginbotham, Suzy Exposito, Leora Tanenbaum, Ann Fessler, Michelle Herrera Mulligan, Sarah Moeller, Tatyana Fazlalizadeh, and Sarah Rankin. Our favorite response to the day was overheard as we waited in line for the bathroom behind two high school freshman: "Alexa, we've been here for four hours already, and I'm not even a little bit bored." Alexa's reply: "Yo, word. I've never had conversations like this before in my life—it's kinda fucking awesome."

To date, StopSlut has reached thousands across the country. From New York City to Los Angeles to Fargo, North Dakota, and beyond, unprecedented conversations among young men and young women, students and teachers, parents and children, film-makers, music producers, social workers, counsel-ors, lawyers, law enforcement, journalists, survivors, and perpetrators are happening.

Doors are opening, truths are being told and heard,

understanding is deepening, solutions are being formed, and best of all, communal catharsis is being achieved from the ground up—young people are jump-starting the communication through custom-tailored events and projects they've developed with their personal energy, passion, and talents. They are leading the charge—as they should. Kids, teens, and young adults live enveloped in this culture every day, they know their hallways, Snapchat stories, and dormitories better than anyone. They are the experts—therefore, the social evolution (the *movement*) required to StopSlut must start with thirteen to twenty-five year olds, with open ears and support from mentors, parents, educators, and community leaders.

"Why StopSlut?" It's a question we get all the time. "Why that name?" Well, StopSlut was coined by two members of The Arts Effect All-Girl Theater Company, Samia and Winnifred. Their reasoning:

> It's simple. Basically, that's what we want. We want a stop to "slutting." We're sick of the permission "slut" gives for harassment, shaming, bullying, aggression, assault, and rape. Don't we have a right to our sexuality—a right to feel safe expressing ourselves sexually? Well, it kinda feels like that right will only be recognized when we stop "slut" and encourage more positive ideas about female sexuality.

It's true. The ability to express one's self sexually is a human right. It's that simple. But like many human rights and civil rights challenges throughout history, the fight to free us all (no matter the gender, age, race, or socioeconomic standing) from the binds of slut culture requires effort (no matter how big or small) from you.

The StopSlut Coalition

The StopSlut Coalition is a worldwide, awareness-raising activist network for young people of all genders. The coalition is committed to ending slut shaming and transforming rape culture into CARE (Communication, Accountability, Respect, and Empathy) culture by igniting positive attitudes toward sexuality through creative, student-driven plans of action. The coalition includes students from middle and high schools and colleges across the country, along with chapter mentors and sponsors. To date, over 1,000 members are participating in local chapters nationwide.

The Coalition has four overarching goals:

1. **BUILD.** Coalition chapters build community by bringing together students and mentors in safe, uncensored environments. As chapters are established, members rely on CARE values to establish the solid infrastructure and a sense of unity needed for the team to engage in effective activism. Open and honest communication ensures the ongoing work of each chapter best meets the unique needs of its members and community.

2. **IDENTIFY.** Coalition chapters identify and breakdown the problems and challenges resulting from slut culture in their specific communities

and beyond, then candidly discuss the impact on young people. Key topics for conversation include: What is rape culture? What is slut shaming? Why do people use the word slut? What are the general effects of slut shaming on the lives of girls and women? And boys and men? Explore the intersectionality of slut beyond gender. Consider race, sexual identity, class, etc. What is the relationship between slut shaming and sexuality, bullying, and rape?

3. **EMPOWER.** Coalition chapter members are empowered through the fusion of knowledge, tools, and collaboration. Each community's efforts to end shaming and sexual violence are strengthened through:
    1. The understanding of the problems and the dreaming of solutions.
    2. The use of members' talents and skills to create sharp custom-tailored, awareness-raising campaigns.
    3. A willingness to collaborate. Chapters embolden their members by offering participants an energized environment to be heard and take action; and empower the outside community providing an opportunity for education, dialogue, and change.

4. **ENGAGE.** The StopSlut Coalition engages youth and motivates movement by acknowledging teens and young adults as the leaders in the fight to end sexual shaming and violence on school campuses, and giving students the tools to develop

unified but diverse plans of action. Teams of coalition members design distinctive activism projects with the common goal of engaging communities in healthy (often unprecedented) conversations about sexuality, bullying, and rape. Each plan serves the specific needs of the university, school, or community center where the chapter is based and comes from the ground up!

The StopSlut Coalition: The Flagship Chapter

The New York City Flagship StopSlut Chapter was established in September 2013 at the first StopSlut Coalition meeting, a precursor to the historic Stop-Slut Conference. Founding members included 125 girls, aged twelve to eighteen years, from each of New York City's five boroughs (Manhattan, Brooklyn, the Bronx, Queens, and Staten Island) and nearby New Jersey communities. The participating students represented twenty-five public, private, and special needs schools. The team was supported by twenty adult mentors from a wide range of areas of expertise and professions. After a day of intensive workshopping, the members hit their hallways on a mission to form individual chapters at their schools. Today, the New York City Chapters consist of over 600 young women and men participating in meetings, clubs, projects, and performances around the city. Whether they are filming their own documentaries, launching school-wide photo campaigns on social media platforms (like "I need feminism because . . ." which reached thousands of students across the country), creating original theatrical pieces, displaying art exhibits, or starting petitions demanding citywide education around consent, the New York City StopSlut activists are inspiring and motivating many in the New York metropolitan area (and beyond) to join the StopSlut Movement.

The following three examples of NYC StopSlut activism illustrate the breadth and impact of the movement's work.

ORIGINAL PERFORMANCE PIECE

Public high school students in Manhattan created a StopSlut chapter within their school. The club grew to involve over twenty-five female and male students. Participants developed a series of original monologues about sexual shaming, sexual aggression, masculinity, femininity, and the need for respect and empathy between genders. The club organized sold-out performances for classmates, friends, family, and the public in locations outside of school, including churches, community centers, and parks. Each showing was followed by an open discussion forum among actors and audience members, and a reception to aid in furthering communication and networking. A participating high school senior offered the following feedback:

> At our school, it's a common thing for teachers to call girls sluts in front of the whole class for violating dress code, so it was kind of surprising that we received school support and were able to hold meetings in school. Even so, we weren't allowed to perform our original theater piece in our HS auditorium, so it forced us to be creative—we per-

formed in a church, a park, and in the basement of a community center. We were blown away by how many friends came out in support. And because we had to hold performances in alternative locations, it meant getting our parents and families involved. We had Q&As after the performances and parents and even grandparents participated. It's important to involve other generations as well. I think the fact that we met some adversity only made our team stronger and, actually, in an interesting way, more appealing to other kids. It made activism seem badass.

SCHOOL SURVEY AND COED DISCUSSION FORUMS

Private high school students in Brooklyn established a StopSlut Chapter in their high school and recruited close to one hundred additional male and female members. Members developed a bullying, sexuality, and gender awareness survey for the middle and high school students and faculty. The results were revealed in a video they created and shared through different social media platforms. They also discussed their findings at a school assembly as part of Women's History Month in March 2014. They continued to have weekly meetings throughout the remainder of the school year—without adults present—to discuss current issues and frustrations. These meetings were strategically planned to be all-girl, all-boy, and in a coming together, all-gender. A fifteen-year-old leader of this chapter shared:

StopSlut has revolutionized our school. Having a space to engage in discussion around the issues of consent, respect, and sexism has been transfor-mative. The administration, at first, was strongly against our club. But we didn't give up and finally found support from guidance counselors and teachers. With our survey, we challenged students and faculty to actually think about their sometimes subconscious actions and come to terms with the way they contribute to slut culture in our commu-nity. I think our biggest accomplishment was our all-gender meeting. I know more was accomplished in those two hours than at any school assembly on bullying, sexual assault, and gender equality. There was honest communication I've never seen—people were genuinely hearing one another.

DOCUMENTARY

Public middle school students in Manhattan estab-lished a StopSlut Chapter outside of school, because they couldn't obtain school approval. Inspired by Humans of New York, this small group of girls took to the streets of Manhattan and interviewed people of all ages and backgrounds about slut shaming and rape culture. They created their own blog, which featured interview videos, essays from girls through-out New York, and links to helpful resources. They used their mini-documentary as the focus of their school current events project and were finally able to screen it in their classroom. A thirteen-year-old eighth grader detailed her experience:

People assume that because we're only in mid-dle school that we're too young to talk about slut shaming and rape, but the truth is it's something we face. Kids start slut shaming in third grade. If you wait until high school to get active with this stuff, it will be too late. When we did our interviews, New Yorkers and tourists were excited to talk to us about the word slut. I think our project shows that slut shaming is not a kid issue, it's something that affects everyone.

It is important to remember that there are countless "right" ways to take action. Your projects may take months to create and implement, or an idea can simply pop into your head, grab the support and attention of friends right off the bat, and be launched into action the next night—as was demonstrated by the members of a Moorhead, Minnesota StopSlut Chapter.

After our StopSlut workshop with a group of Moorhead, Minnesota high schoolers on a Friday afternoon in May of 2014, over seventy students devised an impressive variety of potential action options, but left with one perfect, agreed-upon mission. A simple act of protest would be carried out the next evening. Saturday night. At prom. With the goal of taking a stand against and raising awareness about the glorification of slutting and rape in pop culture, they planned to walk off the dance floor when "Blurred Lines" played (one of the most popular songs in 2013 and littered with rape innuendo), taking as many of their fellow students with them as possible. And they did it. Over 150 young people left the floor. The best part—during the three minute song, students and teachers engaged in conversations about sexist media and the importance of disrupting the cultural status quo. This seemingly small act had massive impact on the Moorhead community, as stated by teacher, Rebecca Meyer-Larson: "What an impact StopSlut immediately made at MHS. I have witnessed, firsthand, girls reframing comments that were once wrapped in slut shaming. I have watched young men call out the double standard of male and female sexuality, and I've seen MHS become a safer place for students because of the vital conversations StopSlut opened up. I am committed to extending this conversation and continuing the mission in our little corner of the universe."

How to Start a StopSlut Chapter in Your Community

A StopSlut Chapter can be established in any way that works for your community. It's important to tailor your chapter to best serve your needs, while also considering your limitations. Here are some quick tips to get you started:

- Find people who are interested. Friends or peers at school, young people in the neighborhood, members of other clubs, faith based institutions, or community organizations.
- Find a mentor. A teacher, professor, or outside professional. If you're in middle or high school, a parent or older sibling can also work. You're looking for someone who can help advocate for your chapter and navigate obstacles you may come across on campus or in your community.
- Find a meeting place. You may decide to meet at your school. Or, if your school is resistant, you

may decide it's best to meet off campus. Obviously, your chapter does not have to be affiliated with an educational institution.

- Begin scheduling timelines and conducting your chapter meetings. For a StopSlut Chapter Meeting Breakdown outlining suggested discussion points and project timeline, visit StopSlut.org.
- Create a mission statement and develop a strategy for recruiting additional members, if needed. Come to a consensus for group communication, planning, and information sharing outside of meetings (e.g., Facebook group, Tumblr page, Instagram, blog, email, or group text).
- Discuss and break down the issues at hand: sexism, slut shaming, sexual harassment, and rape; and the specific challenges facing your community. Use the StopSlut WHAT, HOW, NOW approach.
- Brainstorm plan of action ideas. A plan of action is your plan for activism—the project or initiative you and your team will develop and implement to combat slut shaming and rape culture in your community. Remember: plans of action can come in all shapes, sizes, and mediums—a social media campaign, a film, an art exhibit, a petition, a theatrical piece, an open mic night, or a community walk. Ask yourself: What makes sense for your community? What are your chapter members' strengths? What's the most effective way to raise awareness around issues of sexual shaming, harassment, and violence, while also promoting healthier attitudes toward female sexuality?

WHAT

What is slut culture?

What is slut shaming?

What are some triggers of sexual shaming and rape culture?

What are examples of slut culture that you've collectively witnessed or experienced?

HOW

How does sexual shaming effect young people?

How does the prevalence of slut culture perpetuate rape and sexual assault?

How do people misunderstand the experience of being a young person coming into her or his sexuality in today's world?

NOW

Brainstorm ways people of all genders can own their sexuality freely and healthily.

Give examples of simple things people and communities can do to StopSlut.

- Continue with weekly or bi-weekly meetings as you continue to create and activate your plan.
- Use StopSlut resources. Download the StopSlut Plan of Action Summary and Progress Logs to keep your project on track: StopSlut.org. Remember to keep us and your community updated on your progress: document your journey, post developments to a blog or other social media platform, and stay connected with the StopSlut Coalition.
- Activism can be hard. Ask for help and support from us or others in your community.

Everyday Guide to (Pretty Simple) StopSlut Activism

Maybe plans of action aren't for you. That's fine. You're not the only one. So, how about a checklist? Every day we're asked, "What are some things I can do? Things that are not too time consuming but will still have an impact." Well, here you go! Follow this list and you'll be making an impact daily.

1. STOP USING SLUT. JUST STOP.

And whore, ho, THOT, skank, etc. It might not be easy to kick this bad habit, but the act of extracting this small word from your linguistic diet will have a big impact on you and those around you. The fact is, language matters and the dirtying of female sexuality and limiting of female sexual expression is perpetuated every time someone uses (says, texts, posts, etc.) the word slut. It's true. Even if it's used in jest or in an attempt to reclaim the sexual agency slut traditionally demeans.

You may not believe this, but you will feel better when you stop. You'll be less angry. Your sense of empathy will heighten—you'll start to see people in all their complex glory, rather than as pigeonholed caricatures. You'll be relieved because you, too, will feel safer to make the sexual choices that are right for you.

Think of it this way: saying goodbye to slut is like saying goodbye to a bad friend. She makes you feel bad about yourself, encourages you to turn on others, is possessive, and doesn't let you make your own choices. You've kept her around for so long because it's just easy, familiar, doesn't take too much effort.

We know it's hard but trust us. Once you walk away from her you'll feel free.

So what word should you use instead? Well, here's a question for all of us—why do we need one?

2. CALL 'EM OUT.

Slut is a popular word and people use it frequently in many different contexts. When you hear people say it, call them out. You don't have to bite anyone's head off. Just calmly speak up by saying something like: "'Slut' is a pretty hurtful word—I'm trying not to say it anymore. I'm sure it would mean a lot to people if you stopped saying it too."

Or you can dig deeper: "Why would you call her that?" (We say "her" because it's most often a "her" people are referring to.) "Just curious, what does being a slut mean to you?" "How does that make her a 'slut' exactly?" "Can't she do that if she wants to?"

Remember, tone is very important here—because the goal is a conversation, not a battle. And don't be surprised if you hear these common responses:

"It's just a word, it's not a big deal."

You know that's not true. You can respond with something like: "There are a lot of words we all used to think of as 'No big deal' that we no longer use because we know they're rude, or hateful, or demeaning, you know?" or "It is a big deal actually—it's sexist at its root and words like 'slut' make female sexuality seem like a bad thing when it's not."

"But she is a slut. I mean, she fits the definition in the dictionary, so . . . "

Just because a word is in the dictionary doesn't mean it's one we should use. Slut, from its earliest uses, has been derogatory. It paints the picture of a slovenly, loose, disgusting woman lacking in means and morals—reflecting a history of societal sexual chains that bind female sexuality. You can respond: "So? No matter what, the word reflects antiquated ('old-school') views of female sexuality that have carried over into today's culture—why is it bad that she has sex or even a lot of sex? What's it to you? You may not like it but that doesn't make her bad or evil or dirty or less than."

"You have no sense of humor."

That's a defense mechanism activated because you're calling them out. The bottom line is: sexually shaming someone is never hilarious. Your response: "Oh I definitely do—but my sense of humor is only triggered by things that are actually funny."

"I use it for men too . . . I called guys man-whores.

Your response: "No, you don't." "That doesn't make it better—then you're shaming both sexes for exploring their sexuality. What's the point of that?" "Man-whore still comes with a hint of pride, slut does not—or at least not for long." "The difference between calling a guy a man-whore and a girl a whore or a slut, is that man-whore isn't potentially accompanied with the threat of assault."

In the end, remind yourself that most people use slut for the same reasons you do, they've been conditioned to, they're following societal rules, and they're trying to make sense of things happening in their world. Making them feel like "bad" people will only make them defensive. Most often, the best way to call someone out for using slut is to do it with understanding and curiosity.

3. BACK HER UP.

Being "slutted" is an isolating experience. The victim is often outwardly going through it alone because no one wants to be publicly associated with the slut of the moment for fear of being shamed or humiliated, too. That's the dynamic the slut shamer counts on—it's what gives him or her power and it's the desire for power that most likely triggers the shaming in the first place. Take that power away by backing her up. Offer in-person and online support to girls being slut shamed or trying to take on the issue of slut shaming. When we allow slut shaming to happen to just one person, we are giving permission for this heterosexist attack to strike anyone because slut shaming doesn't discriminate. But permission is a two-way street! When you do take a stand, you give others permission to make themselves heard as well. Unified voices have the strength to shut it down. So, even though it is sometimes a social risk, helping put an end to "slutting" by backing those targeted benefits you and your community in the short and long term. Step in, join the comment thread, speak up!

4. THINK: IS THAT REALLY FUNNY?

We've all heard a rape joke. We've all heard jokes made at the expense of women's bodies and female sexuality. We've probably all laughed. Understandable. We've been taught to find the poking fun of "sluts" and "hos" and women being violated to be "hilarious" and this trope is amplified in the media. Consider: *2 Broke Girls, Work It, Rob, Whitney, Up All Night, Two and a Half Men, Workaholics, Modern Family, It's Always Sunny in Philadelphia, Family Guy, Glee,* and *The Soup* all regularly employ rape jokes; Seth MacFarlane's Oscar speech used women shaming for comedic affect; each October over the past few years, Facebook walls are hit with "Slap a Slut Week." This type of humor has staying power because it works—it almost guarantees a response from the audience. Listeners always chuckle either because they think it's actually funny or because they're afraid of being shamed as "uncool" or "uptight" if they don't. Wonder if this shtick would fade to black if we just stopped laughing? Let's find out!

Whether it's on TV, popping up on your news-feed, or being said by a friend at a party—challenge yourself: Is that joke really funny? And no, you don't need to "lighten up" or "loosen up" or "get over yourself."

Rape and slut shaming are simply not a joke. Making fun of women and girls for being violated or being sexual fuels rape culture.

5. CRITIQUE THE MEDIA.

Beyond cracking jokes, the media makes a practice of sexualizing girls and women and glamorizing sexual violence. From depictions of pimp-ho relation-ships to date-rape-turned-into-love scenarios, from portrayals of women as things to be conquered to painting flirty preteen girls as stupid or evil (aka slutty), the mainstream TV, film, news, video games, and music industries play into and often drive our cultural attitudes toward female sexuality, impacting the millions who consume their products.

And let us not forget the porn industry. The average age a child first sees porn online is estimated to be between eight and eleven years old. Think about it: whether you're male or female, if porn is your first exposure to sex, it's going to have a major impact on your understanding of sexual dynamics.

So what are you supposed to do about it? Be aware and raise awareness. Hold a screening of *Miss Representation* at your house or during a club meeting. Write an op-ed for a local or school paper. And from time to time, boycott. Protest. Turn it off, log off, don't buy the ticket, don't download, and let the producers (and your social circle) know why. Or, even better, create your own content.

6. START A CONVERSATION.

Shifting the tide of sexual shaming and violence begins with conversation. So dare to engage. TALK. Bring these issues out of the dark. Discuss "slutting," consent, street harassment, bystander prevention, rape, you name it, with friends, at a student government meeting, on your Tumblr, or in your column for the campus paper. Remember, these issues touch everyone—most people just don't have the opportunity to open up.

Just recently, a member of the StopSlut Coalition, Eleanor, posted a comment on Facebook about anti-date rape nail polish being developed at North Carolina State University. She said she wished the energy going into the development of an anti-date rape nail polish would be directed toward creating effective anti-date rape education for young people. Within minutes, there were over 200 comments on the thread. Intense debating back and forth between high schoolers about rape, date rape, what is rape, consent, the real world vs. the ideal world, does anti-rape education work, and what does it even mean? While emotionally draining for Eleanor, the exchange happening on her newsfeed was unprecedented and clearly needed within this particular social circle. Was there anger expressed? Yes. Fear? Yes. Were people defensive? Yes. Did everyone agree in the end? No. But, was there communication? Yes. And though not always said in the most "appropriate" ways, everyone on the thread appreciated the threat young women face. Eleanor forwarded us a text from one of the more aggressive boys on the thread that evening: "I know shit got heated last nite on fb and prolly said some shit that offended you. I apologize for that. Want you to know that I respect your views and the fact that you're talking about this stuff."

Creating the space for frank communication about these issues (no matter how heated the dialogue may get) is a gift you can give to your peers, family, and community.

Go for it. Someone has to. Be brave.

7. STAND UP!

What is a bystander? A bystander is a person who is present at an event or incident but does not take part. The young people who attended that party in Steubenville, Ohio, who watched as a young woman was sexually assaulted while passed out drunk, were bystanders. Tim in *SLUT* is a bystander. The best friends of our seventeen-year-old student Anna, who all remained silent on a Facebook thread as she was being slut shamed, were bystanders.

In order to combat sexual shaming and violence, we need people who are equipped to act. We need active bystanders. An active bystander is someone who takes action to make a difference. While observing an incident, being an active bystander involves five steps:

1. Do a "gut check." Is something not right about this?
2. Ask: "Can I play a role?"
3. Think through your options.
4. Contemplate the risks that may come with taking action.
5. Decide whether or not to act in the moment or after the fact.

In all the instances mentioned above, the harm inflicted on the victim would have greatly decreased had the bystanders intervened. Yes, we have a responsibility to ourselves to look out for our own safety and well being—in fact, bystanders often don't speak up or get involved because they genuinely fear losing friendships, retaliation, embarrassing themselves, or making a mistake, and they also tend to think someone else will eventually step in so they won't have to. However, we also have a responsibility to others—if we see someone being targeted, we should be prepared to step in and offer support.

It's crucial to choose the safest form of intervention for you and the victim. Something all of us can do is come up with plans. Role-play, as cheesy as that sounds. Practice. Challenge yourself, your friends, your siblings, and teammates with different hypothetical situations and create game plans for how you'd effectively, safely mediate the conflict.

While there are many options for handling all kinds of situations, here are some strategies to consider:

Identify the offending behavior and create an opportunity for discussion.
"I don't know. I guess I don't find jokes about rape that funny, you know?"

Shine a light on the issue even if everyone else is pretending not to see it.
"Hey, she's had a lot to drink and she shouldn't be going anywhere with anyone right now."

Publicly support the person being targeted.
In-person or online, defend the person being shamed or attacked. Show others you have the back of the person being targeted. More supporters are bound to follow. "Stop calling her a slut. I'm sick of watching you shame my best friend in an attempt to make yourself look big. Enough is enough."

Be friendly—even use humor (but be careful).
"Yo, let me get you another drink. Come on. Over here. Oh and I have this hilarious story I gotta tell

you." "You know she probably doesn't want to dance with you because she's intimidated by your skills."

Use body language to show you don't approve.
In response to slut shaming or tasteless jokes, shake your head, roll your eyes, raise eyebrows, and even walk away.

Intervene and break up the incident.
In Tim's instance, tell the cab driver to pull the cab over. In the Steubenville scenario, guide the drunk young woman to the bathroom because, "She's obviously had too much and needs a break."

Call for help.
Contact law enforcement, a parent, a mentor, a teacher, an older sibling, etc.

Remember there's no one "right" way to be an active bystander. So, try it now. What would you do? Given each of the three examples above (Steubenville, Tim, and online shaming), devise your personal plans of action.

8. KNOW YOUR IX.

Title IX was passed into law for your protection. The provisions under Title IX apply to students of all genders at elementary, middle, and high schools, along with colleges. One of the best ways to protect yourself and hold your school accountable is to Know Your IX.

9. START OR SIGN PETITIONS.

Starting or signing a petition is still an effective way for those in power to hear the voices of the masses. That's why people still do it and that's why sites like change.org are so popular. They allow you to start a petition and make your voice heard by government and business leaders. Encouraging people to sign their name to something engages them—even if in just a small way. It makes them think about an issue and makes their support visible. It's empowering. Well-signed petitions at school or in your community have an impact because they represent people, power, money, and votes.

An impassioned member of the StopSlut Coalition, Max, created a petition entitled Just Hear No to be presented to New York City Mayor Bill DeBlasio. His goal is for the New York City public school system to implement consent education in schools. Max has almost reached his signatures target, but even more importantly, his petition and mission have given his peers a platform to talk and think about consent, and inspired young people throughout New York City to start implementing the motto Just Hear No (and yes means yes) in their own lives—with or without school guidance.

10. IF YOU'RE OVER EIGHTEEN, VOTE.
IF YOU'RE NOT, GET EDUCATED AND EDUCATE OTHERS.

It's never too early to be an active citizen. Voting gives us the opportunity to speak truth to power. You may hear from your uncle or the news media or your favorite podcast that voting means nothing these days. Not true. Passing and enforcing laws can only be done by our elected officials—so it's your responsibility to fight to put people in office who stand up for your rights and help protect your future. Learn about candidates and learn about issues. Politicians care about future voters as well, so if you're under eighteen, don't be shy about reminding them that you'll be voting in a few years and you'll be watching.

Vive La Girl Résistance!

An Afterword with Carol Gilligan

JENNIFER BAUMGARDNER

R aised in New York City, the only child of two first-generation American Jews, Gilligan's 1982 book In a Different Voice provoked a paradigm shift in the human sciences. In it, she demonstrates that qualities associated with women and femininity—empathy, cooperation, relationships—are, in fact, human qualities and human strengths.

I first met Carol Gilligan in 1998, when I interviewed her for Manifesta, my first book (written with Amy Richards). She had just moved to New York University from Harvard and I'd frequently see her strolling around Greenwich Village, wavy brown hair flowing and always with a big, genuine smile. During the summer of 2013, she helped convene a summit to discuss how to support young women. There, she gave a philosophical, rich, and concise definition of feminism. "Feminism is," Gilligan said, "the act of separating patriarchy from democracy." In our conversation, she describes how people resist patriarchal dehumanization every day.

JENNIFER BAUMGARDNER: *What was teen life like for you?*

CAROL GILLIGAN: I grew up in New York at a time when children could wander freely through the city. I went to Hunter Elementary School and at eight, I took two buses to school by myself. We played in Central Park. I went to high school at Walden, a progressive school. I remember biking around the city with my friends. I was involved in the arts. I was involved with sports.

JB: *Sounds rather healthy! When did you first learn about sluts?*

CG: When I was twelve I went to a terrific summer camp in Maine. The junior counselor, who was sixteen and adorable—dark hair, blue eyes—liked me. And it was like wow! He walked me home from campfire and kissed me goodnight. I gained a kind of recognition because this boy was interested in me.

Around that time my mother was trying to teach me what she believed I needed to know about living as a girl. The message was mixed. On the one hand, she said, "trust yourself." At the same time she saw female sexuality as a possession and a gift. I don't think she used the word slut, but she was teaching me about the division of women into good and bad.

JB: *Did religion play into this?*

CG: Judaism is very interesting when it comes to sexuality. Close friends of mine who are Christian have hang-ups around sexuality I never had. My mother taught me that sex is wonderful, beautiful, it's *good*, but you wait until after you're married. I had the sense that I should preserve my virginity as an asset. Once you've lost your virginity you'll never regain your sense of purity or desirability.

JB: *Is that true today?*
CG: No! The sixties changed all of that. When I was in college we had parietal rules: three feet on the floor and the door open two inches. Girls who were married couldn't live in the dorms because they would corrupt the virgins. But the sixties placed sexuality within a much larger questioning of hypocrisy and lies—lies about Vietnam and the hypocrisy about segregation. In that wave of feminism, women's sexuality was celebrated. Shere Hite wrote about female orgasm and we set out to know our own bodies rather than relying on some man to tell us about our sexuality. We could enjoy it and own it. Sexuality wasn't isolated from other ethical questions. I'm interested in freeing sexuality from what Arundhati Roy called "the love laws" of patriarchy, meaning the laws that establish "Who can be loved. And how. And how much." Across time and across cultures, the suppression of an ethically resisting voice has been tied to controlling women's sexuality.

JB: *Why is sexuality so significant to women's experience?*
CG: If you can't know your sexuality then you can't be in your body, and if you can't be in your body, you can't register your experience. Because we regis-

ter our experience in our body and in our emotions. So if you have to dissociate from your sexuality, you have to be outside of your body and then you lose touch with what you know and this has ramifications. First are the psychological effects: eating disorders, cutting, trying to gain control of or feel something in one's body. But there are also political ramifications because if people are dissociated from their experience, their votes will no longer reflect what they know. The girls and guys who are taking on slut culture are onto something that's very important.

JB: *With the young women I talk to, one of the more painful parts of the story for them, particularly when there's a sexual assault and then they're called a slut afterward, is the ways in which other girls are the enforcers.*

CG: Around seventh grade, suddenly, there are the girls whom the boys want to be with and the other girls. A knife cuts through girls' friendships when girls assess each other not on the basis of who is this person, what do I love about her, what do I have in common with her, how much fun do we have together, but how does this person look in the eyes of the world and how will *I* look if I associate with her? You have these terrible games of inclusion and exclusion. It's the initiation of girls. It requires girls to disassociate themselves from their desires and from their own bodies. Once you divide girls, it's easy to silence those who actually speak up. This separation into the good and the bad is enforced by girls, and that's really painful *for* girls.

JB: *I hear often that after rape, many women don't trust other women.*

CG: At a conference in London on preventing HIV/AIDS among adolescents, one of the presenters said that the double standard is really a single standard designed to protect men's vulnerability. Both men and women protect men's vulnerability.

JB: *To being rejected?*

CG: To being shamed. For example, when a man seeks to prove his masculinity by raping a woman, and everybody defends him and protects his masculinity rather than defending the woman and shaming him. What if the question was, "how come if you wanted sex you couldn't find someone who wanted to have sex with you?" Because in a way the rapist is showing his inability to have a woman consent to have sex with him if he has to force it on a woman and prove his masculinity by dominating her.

JB: *I meet a lot of people who would in two seconds call a girl a slut, and really demean her or deny she was assaulted, but if there was a gay bashing incident they would see that as obviously odious.*

CG: In many ways the gender binary hasn't been questioned. What has been promoted—I don't know by whom—as liberation for girls, is to adapt the kind of dissociated sexuality that we used to associate with men. For instance, having sex with no commitment, no relationship, sex dissociated from love, sex for sex, that was seen as sexual freedom. But it was really switching from one side of the binary to the other without questioning the whole structure.

I'm really interested in where girls' voices are in that, what girls can say and girls can't say. Some of the hookup culture reflects young women's awareness of the commitment to being in a relationship with a man. They want the freedom to pursue their own dreams and desires, to have their own lives. So they can have sex without having to take the time and energy it takes to commit to a relationship. But when I asked a friend of mine who's a therapist, what are you seeing these days with the very accomplished women who come into your office, she said she hears this longing for romantic relationships.

JB: *Romantic in what sense? That person will open the door for me and take me out to dinner?*
CG: I don't really know, but I suspect it's something more to do with love. As though the price of freedom was to sacrifice the desire to love and be loved.

In my research that involved listening to girls, when I'd hear a girl say something that sounded memorized, like how you're supposed to think about something, I'd ask the girl: do you really feel that way? And often she'd turn on a dime. "Actually" was the switch word. She would tell me how she "actually" felt, or what she "really" thought, or saw or knew. I'm not sure if that voice is anymore encouraged now than it was in the past, but I'm always listening for that voice in women and girls—the voice that says what she really feels and thinks. It goes way back in the early days of my research. I had asked a woman a question about a moral dilemma and she looked at me and said, "Would you like to know what I think? Or, do you want to know what I really think?" The implication was that she'd learned to think about morality in a way that differed from how she really thought. And it's that voice that I'm always listening for, the *what I really think*.

JB: *How can we make more safe spaces or actually draw that real voice out?*
CG: Be interested in it, be curious about it, and don't just record the first thing a girl or woman says as though that's what she really thinks because we've all learned how we're supposed to think about things, or how we're supposed to feel or what we're supposed to see or listen to or know. So, the voice that says what I really think and feel is often a voice that girls and women hold in silence.

JB: *Is reclaiming slut possible?*
CG: I understand why girls and women try to appropriate the term slut instead of having it used as a weapon against us. "If to be sexual means to be a slut, I'm a slut. Yes I'm sexual. Humans are sexual beings." But there's so much baggage with that word. That word really connotes the splitting of women into the good and the bad, the pure and the impure, the women whom "we" want to be with and those other women who can be used and then discounted or discarded.

My sense is that a girl who claims the word slut to describe herself is claiming the term as more of an "in your face" response to the culture that would shame her than a resistance to the culture.

JB: *Do you mean because it's a slur and shocking and has some defenses associated with it, but it's not a real challenge to sexist culture because it perpetuates the division of women?*

CG: Yes. The sluts are women whom no one protects and women know that. Nobody protects the slut. That means some people can just be used—or worse. Look at honor killings—she can be killed, she can be stoned—and anyone who stands with her is tarnished by that association. To be a slut is dangerous.

JB: *Where are the men in slut culture?*

CG: Well, you have to wonder what has happened to the man or boy who rapes a girl. What has happened to their humanity? So if you see a human being who seemingly has no ability to enter into the experience or feelings of another person, or someone who can rape another person, you have to say, what happened? The bystander is frozen in that moment between being a human—which would mean stepping in, not standing by—and being a member of a culture that sanctions abandoning other people. I mean that's true for the men involved in this and for the women who don't intervene and grab the woman and say, "she's not a slut; you raped her!" When the whole apparatus of the law comes in and says, well, look at the skirt she was wearing, it is the human being who can say, "Wait a minute. She didn't do anything. She likes the feeling of wind on her legs, she felt beautiful," or whatever.

JB: *Where are feminists in slut culture?*

CG: Feminism has sometimes been confused around

VIVE LE GIRL RÉSISTANCE!

this issue. To put it simply, women are humans, women have rights, and women are sexual beings who experience pleasure. All of this flies in the face of patriarchy with its hierarchy that privileges men and its sexual double standard. When feminism focuses on ending men's violence toward women including pornographic violence and the sexual abuse of children, it can become aligned with certain forms of puritanism. And also with man-hating, which can lead young women to say, "I don't want to be associated with that."

I built my book *The Birth of Pleasure* around the myth of Psyche and Cupid, which I read as a map of resistance showing a path that leads to a just and equal relationship between a man and a woman and the birth of a daughter named Pleasure. I was fascinated to discover that our culture has a map and we know the way. When Psyche comes of age, she must resist the trap of becoming an object of others' worship or desire—she must insist on being herself. She is Psyche, a girl, not "new Venus," as others call her—the replica of a goddess. She refuses to be placed on a pedestal. When Cupid disobeys his mother Venus and falls in love with Psyche, he makes her promise never to try to see him in the light or to speak about their love. But for the love story to end not in tragedy but in pleasure, Psyche must break these taboos on seeing her lover and saying what she knows about their love. Because Cupid, who has the reputation of running around and shooting his arrows, is in truth a tender and vulnerable young man. It is only when Psyche breaks the taboo on seeing and speaking about love and

Cupid reveals his love for Psyche, that they can enter into a love that leads to pleasure and a marriage of equals.

Like Psyche, adolescent girls have to resist objectification, however seductive it is. And we have to break all of the prohibitions on seeing and saying what we know through experience about love and about men's vulnerability, meaning their humanness. Otherwise, we're back in an old discourse that problematizes women's sexuality, where you can't see women's desire and you can't speak about men's vulnerability and their tenderness.

JB: *What are ways in which girls resist objectification in real life?*
CG: Girls resist objectification by staying in touch with their bodies and listening for the voice that speaks from experience, as opposed to giving up their voice. They must not dissociate from their own bodies.

JB: *Sounds good, but I feel like I'm still learning how to stay in touch with my body—and I'm forty-four.*
CG: True. We haven't provided role models for young people, necessarily. There was a recent article in the *New York Times* about young women who participate in hookup culture. They work long days and then go out at ten at night to have sex with a hookup buddy, but according to the article, they have to drink before they can do that. Meaning they have to anesthetize themselves. To resist objectification is to act out on the basis of your own desires

and perceptions. Which of course means that you have to be in touch with what you want and know what you see.

Giving girls access to artistic means of expression and encouraging real, meaningful honest relationships among girls and between girls and women, where there is resonance for what they know through experience—these are forms of resistance or ways of joining and educating girls' resistance, as The Arts Effect is doing.

JB: *The point of this book and lifting up this play is to be able to empathize with all of the characters as opposed to getting a lecture or into an argument.*
CG: Art works that way—by relating and connecting. I write plays and novels because association is the only way of undoing dissociation. You can't argue yourself out of dissociation because, as the old saying goes, *you don't know what you don't know.* But you can discover it through an associative process.

JB: *Speaking of creating relationships and associations, the girls and boys that are so far involved in the project have discovered their natural investment in feminism. The more they learn about themselves and what they really think—underneath what the social pressures they face are—the less they use the word slut. They describe it as actually far from something casual, but part of a really deep cycle of diminishing themselves and diminishing other women.*
CG: Slut is the big way of dividing women from

women. Women are a majority of the population in every generation. In a true democracy, women have power. But this power depends on having a voice of our own, meaning a voice that is legitimately connected to the reality of what has happened to us.

StopSlut Glossary

ACTIVE BYSTANDER: Someone who observes an injustice and takes steps to make a difference.[1]

BYSTANDER: Someone who passively observes an injustice and doesn't intervene.

CARE CULTURE: A culture founded on communication, accountability, respect, and empathy.

CONSENT: The affirming of sexual contact through actual language or body language.

CYBERBULLYING: Using social media and the Internet to defame and harass someone, especially to demean and render girls worthless.

FEMINISM: The movement for full political, economic, and social equality of all people.

RAPE: Sexual penetration, no matter how slight, against one's will.[2]

---

1. As defined by MIT's Active Bystander Program.
2. There is no federal, legal definition of rape in the United States.

RAPE CULTURE: A complex set of beliefs that encourage male sexual aggression and supports violence agaisnt women.[3]

SLUT CULTURE: The system through which we practice misogyny in homes and communities. Slut culture ushers in rape, sexual abuse, bullying, and inhumane policing of both genders.

SLUT SHAMING (or **SLUTTING**): Degrading girls' and women's sexuality and using it to justify rape and sexual harrassment.

STOPSLUT: A student-led movement that uses cultural expression to transform rape culture.

---

3. As defined by Emilie Buchwald in her book *Transforming a Rape Culture.*

About the Editors

KATIE CAPPIELLO is a graduate of New York University's Tisch School of the Arts where she studied theater, women's studies, and politics. She is the cofounder and artistic director of The Arts Effect. She has written and codirected four original plays, *Keep Your Eyes Open, FACEBOOK ME, SLUT,* and *A Day in the Life.* In 2010, Katie was honored by the National Women's Hall of Fame for her work with girls worldwide. Originally from Brockton, Massachusetts, Katie currently lives in Brooklyn.

MEG McINERNEY is originally from Bethesda, Maryland, and moved to New York City to attend New York University's Tisch School of the Arts where she studied theater, applied theater, and psychology. In 2007, she cofounded The Arts Effect and now serves as the managing director. She has cocreated and codirected four original plays, *Keep Your Eyes Open, FACEBOOK ME, SLUT,* and *A Day in the Life.* In 2010, Meg was honored by the National Women's Hall of Fame for her work with girls worldwide. Meg currently lives in Manhattan.

About the Contributors

THE ARTS EFFECT ALL-GIRL THEATER COMPANY was founded in 2007 by Katie Cappiello and Meg McInerney as a nurturing, empowering space for ensembles of girls ages eight to eighteen to come together and artistically explore their world. Through a unique combination of intensive acting training, creative writing, debate and discussion, mentorship, and public service, members of The Arts Effect All-Girl Theater Company become change agents—utilizing the power of theater to share their voices, challenge their communities, and inspire their peers. The Arts Effect is dedicated to the development of girl-driven original plays, community events, and on-campus workshops throughout the United Sates and across the globe, all designed to raise awareness and spark open and honest communication about the challenges girls and young women face worldwide. Among others, the company has taken on the issues of the over-sexualization of girls, body image, sex trafficking, and reproductive rights. The Arts Effect All-Girl Theater Company has reached thousands, most notably through the touring of its critically-acclaimed, award-winning plays and supporting workshops: *KEEP YOUR EYES OPEN* ("The Vagina Monologues for Teens!"—*Time Out NY*), *FACEBOOK ME* (CRITIC'S PICK! "A funny yet painfully moving mosaic of coming of age in the digital era."—*BackStage Magazine*), and *SLUT* ("Truthful, raw, immediate!"—Gloria Steinem). Directors Katie Cappiello and Meg McInerney have recently developed Project Impact, a leadership-through-storytelling program for youth sex trafficking survivors, and Generation FREE (devised in collaboration with the Somaly Mam Foundation, Equality Now, and NOW-NYC), an anti-trafficking activism and community-building workshop for New York City teens. The Arts Effect's latest piece *A Day in the Life*, a one-act play that exposes the reality of child sex exploitation in the United States, is currently being performed across the country. The work of The Arts Effect All-Girl Theater Company has been praised by MSNBC, *Teen Vogue*, *New York Magazine*, *Time Magazine*, *CNN*, *Policy Mic*, and more. The Arts Effect was named "The BEST theater program for kids/teens in NYC!" by Nickelodeon/MTV's Parents Connect.

VERONICA ARREOLA is a professional feminist, writer, and mom. By day, she directs a women-in-science-and-engineering program, and by night, she is a freelance writer who has been blogging since the turn of the century. vivalafeminista.com

JENNIFER BAUMGARDNER is the executive director and publisher of the Feminist Press. She is the author of *Manifesta: Young Women, Feminism, and the Future*, *Grassroots: A Field Guide for Feminist Activism*, *Look Both Ways: Bisexual Politics*, *Abortion & Life*, and *F' em!: Goo Goo, Gaga, and Some Thoughts on Balls*. Jennifer is also the creator of the *I Had an Abortion* project and film, as well as the director and producer of *It Was Rape*. She writes frequently for magazines ranging from *Harper's Bazaar* to *The Nation*, is the cocreator of Feminist Camp and Soapbox Inc. (a feminist speakers' bureau), and she travels the country talking about activism, feminism, and the crucial experiences that we're supposed to keep secret.

SORAYA CHEMALY is a media critic and feminist activist whose work focuses on the role that gender plays in politics, religion, education, and more. She writes particularly about the role that sexualized violence and sexual entitlement play in gender-based discrimination and hate. Her work appears in *Time*, *Salon*, *The Nation*, *The Guardian*, and others. sorayachemaly.tumblr.com

DUANE de FOUR is an educator, media critic, and activist specializing in gender violence prevention, bystander intervention, and sexual health education. In twenty years as an educator, he has facilitated thousands of trainings at colleges and universities across the country, the NFL, NBA, NHL, NASCAR, and the US Marine Corps, Army, Air Force, and Air National Guard. You can read more of his writing at HowManly.com.

CAROL GILLIGAN is a prominent feminist ethicist, psychologist, and a professor at New York University. She is a highly influential voice in the expansion of psychology to include female development and the founder of the girls' movement. Her published works include the groundbreaking book *In A Different Voice*, the novel *Kyra*, and most recently, *Joining the Resistance*.

YASMEEN HASSAN is the global director of Equality Now, an international human rights organization that works to protect and promote the rights of women and girls globally. She is a Harvard-educated lawyer with more than twenty years of experience in international women's rights, with a special focus on rights under Islamic law. Ms. Hassan is a native of Pakistan and the mother of two sons.

JOHN KELLY is a Tufts University senior majoring in religion and an ED ACT NOW and special projects organizer for the grassroots campaign Know Your IX, which works to combat campus sexual violence. He is a queer survivor of intimate partner violence and rape, and in June of 2014 became the first person to ever testify before Congress on same-sex dating violence.

ILEANA JIMÉNEZ is the founder of the blog, Feminist Teacher. For the past eighteen years, Ileana has been a leader in the field of social justice education. Based in New York, Ileana teaches innovative and award-winning courses on feminist and queer issues that have gained the attention of education and activist circles.

SARAH RANKIN recently became the Title IX investigator for MIT where she investigates cases of sexual assault, sexual harassment, relationship violence, and stalking. Formerly, she was the director of Harvard University's Office of Sexual Assault Prevention and Response for seven years and spent six years as the campus victim advocate at Western Washington University. She has coordinated large peer education programs on both campuses focused on sexual assault prevention efforts.

LEORA TANENBAUM is the author of five books including *I Am Not a Slut: Slut-Shaming in the Age of the Internet* and *Slut! Growing Up Female with a Bad Reputation*. She coined the term "slut-bashing" and helped develop the language that describes slut shaming.

FARAH TANIS is the cofounder and executive director of Black Women's Blueprint and the Museum of Women's Resistance (museumofwomensresistance. org). Tanis also chairs the US Truth and Reconciliation Commission on Black Women and Sexual Assault (myfreedomlounge.com).

JAMIA WILSON is the executive director of YTH, a nonprofit organization that advances youth, health, and wellness through technology. In addition to serving as a staff writer for *Rookie*, she is a contributor to several anthologies including *Women, Spirituality, and Transformative Leadership: Where Grace Meets Power; Rookie: Yearbook's One, Two, and Three, Our Bodies, Ourselves* (2011 Edition), *Madonna and Me: Women Writers on the Queen of Pop* and *I Still Believe Anita Hill*. jamiawilson.com

Acknowledgments

O ur work, particularly this three-year *SLUT* journey, has been possible thanks to the amazing
support from family, friends, students, mentors,
teachers, and collaborators.

First and foremost, we want to thank our awesome parents, Jane and Mike Cappiello and Claudia
and Maury McInerney for believing in us, encouraging us to take risks, and inspiring us to become
the women and teachers we are today. Thank you to
our loving, loyal siblings Jim and Mariko Cappiello,
Scott and Patty Erker, Ann Nicocelli, and Stephen
and Ashley McInerney. The greatest in-laws *ever*:
the Tilsners (Gail, Tommy, Jodi, Gregg, Jeremy, and
Rachael) and the Kunkas (Jacquie, Joe, Peter, and
Jaimee). Our dear friends, near and far, who have
our backs always: Chrissy Cogan, Dana Villarreal,
Jenny Chiu, Justin Trificana, Nancy Ting, Sasithon
Pooviriyakul, Shirin Shabdin, Jordan and Lindsey
Greenberger, Sue, Brenden, and Stella Fitzgerald,
Nancy, Eric, Matty and Ali Chilton, Sarah Haag-Fisk,
and Lana Underwood House.

We have the best job in the world and we are indescribably proud of our students at The Arts Effect—in particular, the members of The Arts Effect All-Girl Theater Company, who every week are committed to telling important, often unheard truths through art. Your bravery, strength, dedication, and leadership is changing the world. We are in awe! Thank you to the parents as well. Your trust, collaboration, and community continue to mean so much to us.

A very special *thank you* to one of our heroes and favorite people, Jennifer Baumgardner, for responding to our fangirl email all those years ago and being a motivating teammate ever since! Every day we appreciate your talent, advice, guidance, humor, and your passion for this project. We are very lucky to have you in our lives as a colleague (dream come true!) and a friend.

Thanks to everyone at the Feminist Press including: JB, the brilliant, unstoppable Taryn Mann, Yamberlie Tavarez, Julia Berner-Tobin, Drew Stevens, Jisu Kim, Elizabeth Koke, Nino Testa, the devoted board members, and the talented interns. We feel honored to have found a home at such a historic, trailblazing, empowering publishing house. We are grateful for the energy and time that went into making this project a reality.

A shout-out in admiration to the contributors of this book! Women and men we deeply admire: Veronica Arreola, Soraya Chemaly, Duane de Four, Carol Gilligan, Yasmeen Hassan, Ileana Jiménez, John Kelly, Sarah Rankin, Leora Tanenbaum, Farah Tanis, and Jamia Wilson. We're thrilled to have you on our

ACKNOWLEDGMENTS

team and we're proud to be in the trenches with you game-changing activists. Thank you for offering your refreshing insights and dynamic voices.

To the bold young people who share their personal stories in this publication and at StopSlut events across the country, thank you for being you, putting the truth out there, and sparking much-needed conversations. You all courageously exemplify the importance of storytelling and the beauty of vulnerability.

We don't know where we'd be without the love and personal and professional investment from Elizabeth Cuthrell, David Urrutia, and Jeremy Bloom of Evenstar Films. Thank you for believing in the importance of *SLUT* from the very beginning, helping us share this story, and supporting our vision.

Oh, Lauren Hersh! Our fierce friend and soul sister! You motivated Katie to finish the damn script, read the play scene by scene, time and time again, and offered invaluable insight into the legal procedures around sexual assault. THANK YOU!

Yasmeen Hassan and everyone at Equality Now, thank you for believing theater plays an essential role in social change and hosting the first staged reading of *SLUT*. We cherish our continued partnership with you.

Thank you to the New York International Fringe Festival and Elena Holy for giving *SLUT* its first run and supporting the voices of young, up-and-coming artists. And to Darren Cole of the Soho Playhouse and Players Theater for believing this play deserved an "encore!"

We are filled to the brim with gratitude for our gifted technical design team led by Daniel Melnick: Niki Armato, Alejandro Fajardo, Gemma Kaneko, Grant McDonald (extra special thank you to you, GM), Janelle Richardson, Jenn Tash, and Laurie Seifert Williams. We are in awe of your talent, ingenuity, and ability to surmount any technical challenge whether in a theater, art gallery, or high school auditorium! Thank you for being endlessly kind to the cast and us (even on those high-stress days).

Karen Stoker, Susan Smalley, and Kevin Wall, you are the dream makers! Your generosity made it possible for this play and movement to reach thousands across the country. We are forever grateful for and moved by your willingness to take leaps and your commitment to social justice. Thank you also to Claudia Bestor and everyone at the Hammer Museum in Los Angeles, Savannah Badalich, Maria Bello, Amanda de Cadenet, La Shonda Coleman and her team at the Rape Treatment Center at Santa Monica-UCLA, Michelle Czarnik, Torrey DeVitto, Nikki and Josh Donen, Bethany Joy Lenz, Mary and Matt McCoy, and Daphne Zuniga. To everyone at North Dakota State University, Rebecca Meyer-Larson and staff and students at Moorhead High School, Mark Weiler and Ecce Art Gallery, and Kent Kolstad and Livewire Entertainment.

Thank you to the New School, Karen Noyes, Soapbox, Inc., Equality Now, and St. Francis College for hosting StopSlut: A Conference on Sexuality, Bullying, and Rape. We deeply appreciate the event's dynamic panelists and speakers: Lisa Brunner, Christen Clifford, Michaela Angela Davis,

Suzy Exposito, Tatyana Fazlalizadeh, Ann Fessler, Anastasia Higginbotham, Emily May, Sarah Moeller, Michelle Herrera Mulligan, Sarah Rankin, Amy Richards, Leora Tanenbaum, Wagatwe Sara Wanjuki, and Jamia Wilson.

We are inspired by the members' work of the StopSlut Coalition and the nurturing, giving, radiant mentors who offered their time and expertise in support of the student-led chapters: Laura Barnett, Jessica Bennett, Shira Rose Berk, Corey Calabrese, Elizabeth Cuthrell, Dorcas Davis, Christina Liu, Kathy Najimy, Allison Palmer, Bree Person, Lydia Pilcher, Molly Olsen, and Julianne Ross.

To Gloria Steinem for being a hero and always being present. To the wonderful women and men we consider mentors and friends: Bill Balzac, Grace A. Blake, Diane Hardin, Geoffrey Horne, Judy Katz, Bob Marks, Kathy Najimy, Amy Richards, and Rachel Simmons. Thank you for the revolutionary work you do and the coffee dates, conference calls, email exchanges, performance opportunities, and words of wisdom that helped us get here.

What a gift it is to have such a kick-ass Arts Effect teaching team. Charlotte Arnoux, Jon Sokolow, and Jamie Wolfe, thank you for your talent, creativity and kindness, and for being so good to the kids. Thank you also to Phoenix Skye Maulella, Marie Stefania, Ilanna Tariff, and India Witkin for being the best interns we could ever ask for.

To Rich Bart and AJBart Printing, along with our talented graphic/web designer Jeremi Chenier—your stunning work has been the face of this project. We appreciate you so!

Much love to our patient, hilarious, protective, very feminist agent (and buddy!) Scott Yoselow and everyone at The Gersh Agency, especially Sophie Klein and Corinne Greco.

Thank you to Brockton High School especially Katie's inspirational teachers: Penny Aschuler, Carol Thomas, James Burley, Dr. and Mr. Szachowitz; and Bethesda-Chevy Chase High School, especially Meg's life-changing teachers: Sandra Geddes, Sherion Cosby, and Matthew Boswell. Thank you to New York University and Tisch School of The Arts.

To the audiences across the country, who were daring enough to come see a play called *SLUT* and then started talking, a HUGE thank you.

Finally, we want to thank our significant others, Jamison Tilsner and Jason Kunka. Thank you for listening, reading drafts late into the night, cooking dinners, making us laugh, troubleshooting, sitting in the audience together show after show (and clapping the loudest), encouraging us to be our best and bravest selves, reminding us to "just go for it," for being our travel buddies, awesome feminist partners, our rocks, and biggest fans. Thanks for your ceaseless love and abundance of support. We love you.

The Feminist Press promotes voices on the margins of dominant culture and publishes feminist works from around the world, inspiring personal transformation and social justice. We believe that books have the power to shift culture, and create a society free of violence, sexism, homophobia, racism, cis-supremacy, classism, sizeism, ableism and other forms of dehumanization. Our books and programs engage, educate, and entertain.

See our complete list of books at
feministpress.org

THE FEMINIST PRESS
AT THE CITY UNIVERSITY OF NEW YORK
FEMINISTPRESS.ORG